RAISING
ARIZONA

RAISING ARIZONA

An Original Screenplay by

JOEL COEN
and
ETHAN COEN

St. Martin's Griffin
New York

Design by Judith Stagnitto

Front cover photo and photos in text by Melinda Sue Gordon

Library of Congress Cataloging-in-Publication Data

Coen, Joel.
  Raising Arizona / Joel and Ethan Coen.
    p.   cm. — (St. Martin's original screenplay series)
  Screenplay for the motion picture Raising Arizona.
  ISBN 0-312-02270-0
  I. Coen, Ethan. II. Raising Arizona (Motion picture) III. Title.
  IV. Series.
PN1997.R2257 1988
791.43'72—dc19   88-12019
                                                             CIP

10 9 8 7 6

Raising Arizona and *Evil Dead II:*

A Colloquium

In March of 1986 *Raising Arizona*, a feel-good movie about
cute little babies, and *Evil Dead II: Dead by Dawn*, a feel-
good splatter movie, had their commercial openings on
the same day. In order to illuminate other similarities between the two pictures, Joel and Ethan Coen, the authors
of the first movie, chatted with their friends Sam Raimi,
Robert Tapert, and Bruce Campbell, respectively the di-
rector, producer, and star of the second.

Joel: We very much enjoyed *Evil Dead II: Dead by
         Dawn.*
Rob: Thank you.
Ethan: Our hats are off to you!
Bruce: Thanks. We enjoyed *Raising Arizona.*
Ethan: We congratulate you!
Sam: Thanks.
Ethan: You boys did a remarkable job. *Evil Dead II* is a
         great picture by anybody's—according to any-
         one you ask. Everyone says it's a great picture—
         and it is!
Bruce: Thank you, thanks a lot.
Joel: As you know, our picture just came out also,
         Raising Arizona—
Rob: And that was a great picture!

Joel:	Uh-huh. And not just according to you, but according to lots of other people too. Throughout the entire industry, and the public at large.
Bruce:	Well you deserve all the praise in the world for that picture.
Joel:	Uh-huh.
Ethan:	So *Evil Dead II*. How did you do it? How did—all the effects, the complicated camera stuff?
Sam:	Actually it was—
Ethan:	Was it a team effort?
Rob:	You surround yourself with people who—
Joel:	So you're saying, Yes, it was a team effort?
Rob:	Okay, yeah—
Joel:	Our picture was a team effort too. That aspect of it was highly praised. But do you want to know something?
Rob:	Sure.
Joel:	In our picture, the main couple, who live in a trailer—that trailer was all built on a sound stage. It was totally fake.
Sam:	Yeah, well the cabin in our picture, where all the action takes place, we built that on a stage too.
Joel:	Big deal, everyone does that.
Sam:	Yeah—
Ethan:	In the olden days, in Hollywood, almost all pictures were all shot inside on a stage and stuff. Also they had the star system and big producers like Irving J. Thalberg.
Bruce:	Yeah, I know.
Joel:	How do you respond when people accuse your pictures of being grand guignol?
Bruce:	Well it's not a criticism, it's not a negative thing.
Joel:	It is so. Don't you know what grand guignol is? They're not saying your picture is grand, like the Freddy pictures are just plain guignol but your pictures are *grand* guignol. It's all just one thing, grandguignol. It goes together.

Bruce: Yeah but it doesn't mean something bad or derogatory. It just means that they're sort of gory and fun.

Joel: It does?

Bruce: Yeah.

Ethan: Well congratulations on your achievement! We thought *Evil Dead II: Dead by Dawn* was a great picture. But do you want to know something? A lot of it was fakey. Like that scene where the dead woman danced around under her decapitated head? Totally fakey. That couldn't happen.

Rob: I think it's a question of fantasy. It's not supposed to be like real life.

Ethan: But you never said that! You never say that in the movie!

Joel: You never said it!

Sam: But people know, from the advertising and stuff, they know the kind of movie—

Bruce: What about *your* movie? You have a biker blow a lizard off a rock, from a moving motorcycle, from like 200 feet away—

Ethan: That's different.

Bruce: It's a movie!

Joel: That's different. That could happen. A guy on a motorcycle, if he's a good shot, plenty of practice and so forth, he could do that. Maybe not hit the lizard every time, but it's possible. We just had him do it once. If everything breaks the right way, it's possible. Whereas in your picture, the dancing around with no head, even if everything broke right, no.

Sam: It's a fantasy—

Joel: Well I guess that's as good a cop-out as any.

Ethan: What are the themes of your picture?

Sam: Well it doesn't really . . . it's just entertainment.

Ethan: Yeah, but what are the themes? Like ours, we

had, family life versus being an outlaw. What was yours?

Rob: I guess you could say good versus evil—Bruce's character, Ash, being good, against the forces of evil.

Ethan: Sounds pretty heavy for an entertainment picture.

Bruce: Well it was treated with a light touch.

Joel: We treated ours with a light touch also. Many people have commented on that, in the many publications which ran big stories about our picture.

Ethan: Do you like message pictures?

Rob: I, uh . . . I like a picture with a good message.

Ethan: Would you go to see a message picture or a Freddy picture? If they were both playing at the same time.

Joel: If you could only see one.

Rob: Well, like, what's the message picture?

Ethan: *Guess Who's Coming to Dinner.*

Rob: . . . God, I don't know.

Ethan: How about a message picture or a really good meal?

Joel: With all the trimmings.

Ethan: Somebody else paying.

Rob: I don't . . . I . . .

Ethan: Sam, how about you?

Sam: I don't . . . what would *you* pick?

Joel: The message picture.

Ethan: Congratulations again on *Evil Dead II: Dead by Dawn!*

Bruce: Thanks—

Ethan: We gotta go.

Joel: We're interviewing Coppola.

Credits

The Players

H.I.	Nicolas Cage
Ed	Holly Hunter
Nathan Arizona Sr.	Trey Wilson
Gale	John Goodman
Evelle	William Forsythe
Glen	Sam McMurray
Dot	Frances McDormand
Leonard Smalls	Randall "Tex" Cobb
Nathan Junior	T. J. Kuhn
Florence Arizona	Lynne Dumin Kitei
Prison Counselor	Peter Benedek
Nice Old Grocery Man	Charles "Lew" Smith
Younger FBI Agent	Warren Keith
Older FBI Agent	Henry Kendrick
Ear-Bending Cellmate	Sidney Dawson
Parole Board Chairman	Richard Blake
Parole Board Members	Troy Nabors
	Mary Seibel
Hayseed in the Pickup	John O'Donnal
Whitey	Keith Jandacek
Minister	Warren Forsythe
"Trapped" Convict	Ruben Young
Policemen in Arizona House	Dennis Sullivan
	Dick Alexander
Feisty Hayseed	Rusty Lee
Fingerprint Technician	James Yeater

Reporters	Bill Andres
	Carver Barnes
Unpainted Secretary	Margaret H. McCormack
Newscaster	Bill Rocz
Payroll Cashier	Mary F. Glenn
Scamp with Squirt Gun	Jeremy Babendure
Adoption Agent	Bill Dobbins
Gynecologist	Ralph Norton
Mopping Convict	Henry Tank
Supermarket Manager	Frank Outlaw
Varsity Nathan Jr.	Todd Michael Rogers
Machine Shop Earbender	M. Emmet Walsh
Glen and Dot's Kids	Robert Gray
	Katie Thrasher
	Derek Russell
	Nicole Russell
	Zachary Sanders
	Noell Sanders
Arizona Quints	Cody Ranger
	Jeremy Arendt
	Ashley Hammon
	Crystal Hiller
	Olivia Hughes
	Emily Malin
	Melanie Malin
	Craig McLaughlin
	Adam Savageau
	Benjamin Savageau
	David Schneider
	Michael Stewart

and Featuring the Amazing Voice of William Preston Robertson

Directed by	Joel Coen
Produced by	Ethan Coen
Written by	Ethan Coen and Joel Coen
Co-Produced by	Mark Silverman
Executive Producer	James Jacks
Associate Producer	Deborah Reinisch
Director of Photography	Barry Sonnenfeld
Production Designer	Jane Musky

Edited by	Michael R. Miller
Music by	Carter Burwell
Costume Designer	Richard Hornung
Supervising Sound Editor	Skip Lievsay
Associate Editor	Arnold Glassman
Casting by	Donna Isaacson C.S.A.
	and John Lyons C.S.A.
Stunt Coordinator	Jery Hewitt
Stunt Players	Jery Hewitt
	Bill Anagnos
	Curt Bortel
	Shane Dixon
	Allan Graf
	Cindy Wills Hartline
	Gene Hartline
	Jeff Jensen
	Edgard Mourino
	Ron Nix
	Spanky Spangler
Production Manager	Kevin Dowd
Production Supervisor	Alma Kutruff
Production Auditor	Barbara-Ann Stein
First Asst. Directors	Deborah Reinisch
	Kelly Van Horn
Second Asst. Directors	Jon Kilik
	Patricia Doherty
	Chitra Mojtabai
Location Manager	David Pomier
Prod. Office Coordinators	Christopher Buchanan
	Sharon Roesler
Second Unit and Post-Prod. Manager	Andrew Sears
Assistant Auditor	Laura McGillicuddy
Camera Operator	David M. Dunlap
Assistant Camera	Richard P. Crudo
	C. Mitchell Amundsen
Camera Dept. Asst.	Brad S. Mudgett
Steadicam Operator	Stephen St. John
Prod. Still Photographer	Melinda Sue Gordon
Production Sound Mixer	Allan Byer
Boom Operator	Peter F. Kurland
Additional Boom	Randy Gable
Recordist	Greg Horn

Re-Recording Mixer	Mel Zelniker
Key Grip/Dolly Grip	Dennis Gamiello
Rigging Grip	John "Earl" Lowry
Best Boy Grip	Brian Fitzsimmons
Grips	Cindy Lagerstrom
	Bob Preston
	Marty Miller
	Tom Dreesen
Gaffer	Russell Engels
Best Boy	Kenneth R. Conners
First Electric	Michael Burke
Electricians	Bob Field
	George Ball
	Dan MacCallum
	Craig Woodruff
	Michael Hall
Art Director	Harold Thrasher
Set Decorator/Draftsperson	Robert Kracik
Key Set Dresser	Marcia Calosio-Foeldi
Set Dressers	Roger Belk
	Chris Russchon
	Linette Forbes Shorr
Construction Coord.	Stephen Roll
Lead Carpenter	Terry Kempf
Carpenters	Pasco Di Carlo
	Star Fields
	Bill Holmquist
	Bill Seifried
	Chuck Seifried
Scenic Artists	Mark Donnelly
	Todd Hatfield
Storyboard Artist	J. Todd Anderson
Make-up	Katharine James-Cosburn
Hair	Dan Frey
Asst. to Costume Designer	Ellen M. Ryba
Wardrobe Supervisor	Stephen M. Chudej
Wardrobe Assistants	Wendy Cracchiolo
	Ada Akaji
	Brian Kirk
Costume Construction	Mary Ann Ahern
Hair and Make-up Assistant	Camille Henderson

Property Master	Roger Pancake
Asst. Property Master	Jan Fead
Property Man	Britt Torney
Special Effects	Image Engineering, Inc.
Special Effects Coord.	Peter Chesney
Special Effects Lead	Guy Louthan
Animal Action by	Karl Lewis Miller
Arizona Casting	Sunny Seibel
Extras Casting	Becca Korby-Sullivan
Baby Casting	Yvonne Van Orden and Joseph Schneider, Inc., New York City
Baby Wrangler	Julie Asch
Dialect Coach	Julie Adams
Sound Editors	Philip Stockton
	Magdaline Volaitis
	Ron Bochar
First Asst. Editor	Michael Berenbaum
Asst. Editor	Kathie Weaver
Asst. Sound Editors	Bruce Pross
	Marissa Littlefield
	Steven Visscher
	Christopher Weir
Apprentice Editor	Brian Johnson
Script Supervisor	Thomas Johnston
A. D. Production Assts.	Maureen Hymers
	Erin Stewart
	Eric Tignini
Production Secretary	Valerie Susan Brown
Location Assistant	Adam Grad
Location Prod. Assts.	Rick Ashman
	Matt Cartsonis
	L. R. Kelly
	Kim Seeger
Art Dept. Assts.	John Anderson
	Flint Esquerra
	Robb Roetman
	Katie Tansley
	Gerry Thrasher
Office Assistant	Blake Hocevar
Craft Services	Bob Childers
	Elizabeth Boyd

Special Electronic Sound Effects	Frederick Szymanski
	Jun Mizumachi
	Carl Mandelbaum
Foley Artist	Marko A. Constanzo
Foley Engineer	Michael Barry
Dolby Consultant	Michael DiCosimo
Negative Cutting	J. G. Films, Inc.
Title design by	Dan Perri
Music Engineering	Sebastian Niessen
Banjo	Ben Freed
Jews Harp, Guitar	Mieczyslaw Litwinski
Yodeling	John R. Crowder
Digital Score Assistant	Dan Conte

Special thanks to:

Dick Bowers

Office of the Mayor and City Manager, City of Scottsdale, Arizona

Phoenix Motion Picture/Commercial Coordinating Office

Arizona Film Commission

Carol Porter

Short Stop Markets

A Cardon Company, Tempe, Arizona

Home Depot Stores

Golden Horseshoe Stables, Scottsdale, Arizona

Happy Valley Landscape Supply

Dom Masters

Kurt Woolner

Susan Rose

Indian Jewelry Courtesy of Gilbert Ortega Fine Indian Jewelry

Reata Pass Steak House, Scottsdale, Arizona

Señor Greaser

Dental Work Courtesy of Dr. Gary M. Johnson

Eyewear Courtesy of Dr. Berton Siegel, O.D.D.O.

John Raffo

Portions of this picture were filmed in the Tonto National Forest, Forest Service, U.S. Department of Agriculture

Lighting and Grip Equipment Supplied by GENERAL CAMERA WEST, Los Angeles

Lenses and Panaflex Camera by PANAVISION Supplied by GENERAL CAMERA EAST, New York

Color by DuART

Post Production Services by SOUND ONE and THE SPERA CORPORATION

Opticals by THE OPTICAL HOUSE, New York

This picture was shot on location in Arizona's Valley of the Sun
   A Great Place to Raise Your Kids

RAISING ARIZONA

OVER BLACK:

VOICE-OVER: My name is H. I. McDunnough . . .

A WALL

With horizontal hatch lines.

VOICE-OVER: . . . Call me Hi.

A disheveled young man in a gaily colored Hawaiian shirt is launched into frame by someone offscreen.
He holds a printed paddle that reads "NO. 1468-6 NOV 29 79."
The hatch marks on the wall behind him are apparently height markers.

VOICE-OVER: . . . The first time I met Ed was in the county lock-up in Tempe, Arizona . . .

FLASH

As his picture is taken.

CLOSE UP

On the paddle: "NOV 29 79."

VOICE-OVER: . . . a day I'll never forget.

A bellowing male voice from offscreen:

SHERIFF: Don't forget the profile, Ed!

ANGLE ON THE STILL CAMERA

It is mounted on a tripod. A pretty young woman in a severe police uniform peers out from behind it.

WOMAN: Turn to the right.

HI: What kind of name is Ed for a pretty thing like you?

ED: Short for Edwinna. Turn to the right!

HI obliges, but still looks at ED out of the corner of his eye.

HI: You're a flower, you are. Just a little desert flower.

FLASH

On his eye-skewed profile.

HI: Lemme know how those come out.

LOW ANGLE   CELL BLOCK CORRIDOR

As HI is escorted away from the camera toward his cell.
  At the far end of the corridor a huge CON is sluggishly mopping the floor.

VOICE-OVER: I was in for writing hot checks which, when businessmen do it, is called an overdraft. I'm not complainin', mind you; just sayin' there ain't no pancake so thin it ain't got two sides. Now prison life is very structured—more than most people care for . . .

INTERCUTTING

HI's POV of the MOPPING CON, *tracking as he approaches, and the* MOPPING CON's *POV of* HI *as* HI *approaches.*

VO: . . . But there's a spirit of camaraderie that exists between the men, like you find only in combat maybe . . .

The MOPPING CON *snarls as* HI *passes:*

CON: Grrrr . . .

VO: . . . or on a pro ball club in the heat of a pennant drive.

NEWSREEL FOOTAGE

A ballplayer connects—THWOCK—for a home run and the crowd roars.

Nicolas Cage (Hi) in center

PRISON HALL

Panning a circle of men who sit facing each other in folding chairs. The pan starts on HI.

VO: In an effort to better ourselves we were forced to meet with a counselor who tried to help us figure out why we were the way we were . . .

At this point the pan has reached the COUNSELOR, *an earnest, bearded young man who straddles a folding chair with his arms folded over its back.*
  He is addressing one of the cons:

COUNSELOR: Why do you use the word "trapped"?

CLOSE UP   BLACK CON

The huge muscle-bound black man with a shaved head is knitting his brow in consternation.

CON: Huh?

COUNSELOR: Why do you say you feel "trapped" . . . in a man's body?

CON: Oh . . .

He bites his lip, thinking; then, in a resonant bass voice:

. . . Well, sometimes I get the menstrual cramps real hard.

PAROLE MEETING ROOM

Three PAROLE OFFICERS—*two men and a woman—face* HI *across a table.*

CHAIRMAN: Have you learned anything, Hi?

HI: Yessir, you bet.

WOMAN: You wouldn't lie to us, would you Hi?

HI: No ma'am, hope to say.

CHAIRMAN: Okay then.

EXT 7-ELEVEN NIGHT

A beat-up Chevy pulls into the all-night store's empty parking lot.

VO: I tried to stand up and fly straight, but it wasn't easy with that sumbitch Reagan in the White House . . .

HI is getting out of the Chevy in a Hawaiian shirt, holding a pump-action shotgun.

. . . I dunno, they say he's a decent man, so . . .

He primes the shotgun—WHOOSH-CLACK—and heads for the store.

. . . maybe his advisers are confused.

FLASH

Full-face exposure of HI once again in front of the mug-shot wall.

ED: Turn to the right!

HI obliges but shoots sympathetic glances at ED who is obviously upset, wiping away tears and snuffling behind the camera.

HI: What's the matter, Ed?

ED: My fai-ants left me.

VO: She said her fiancé had run off with a student cosmetologist who knew how to ply her feminine wiles.

FLASH

On HI's profile. He turns back to ED.

HI: That sumbitch.

SHERIFF (*offscreen*):   Don't forget his phone call, Ed!

HI: You tell him I think he's a damn fool, Ed. You tell him *I* said so—H. I. McDunnough. And if he wants to discuss it he knows where to find me . . .

As another police officer starts to lead him away:

HI: . . . in the Munroe County Maximum Security Correctional Facility for Men . . .

CLOSE ON ED

Looking up through her tears as HI is led away.

HI (*os*):   . . . State Farm Road Number Thirty-one; Tempe, Arizona . . .

BACK TO HI

Struggling to call back over his shoulder as he is firmly led out the door.

HI: . . . I'll be waiting!

The door slams.

LOW ANGLE   CELL BLOCK CORRIDOR

As HI is once again escorted toward his cell.
The MOPPING CON is now in the middle-background,
having worked his way about halfway up the corridor since
last time we saw him.

VO: I can't say I was happy to be back inside, but the
flood of familiar sights, sounds and faces almost made it
feel like a homecoming.

CLOSE ON MOPPING CON

As HI passes.

CON: Grrrr . . .

PRISON HALL

Group is meeting again.

COUNSELOR: Most men your age, Hi, are getting
married and raising up a family. They wouldn't accept
prison as a substitute.

HI looks sheepish.

COUNSELOR: . . . Would any of you men care to
comment?

Two convicts sitting next to each other, GALE and EVELLE,
appear to be friends.

GALE: But sometimes your career gotta come before
family.

EVELLE: Work is what's kept *us* happy.

ANGRY BLACK CON: Yeah, but Doc Schwartz is sayin'
you gotta accept responsibilities. I mean I'm proud to say
I got a family . . . somewheres.

HIGH ANGLE CELL

*Looking down from the ceiling. In the foreground, lying on
the top bunk, hands clasped behind his head as he stares off
into space is* MOSES. MOSES *is a gnarled, elderly black con
with wire-rimmed spectacles.*
    *On the lower bunk, also with hands clasped behind his
head and staring off at the same spot in space, is* HI.

VO: I tried to sort through what the Doc had said, but
prison ain't the easiest place to think.

MOSES: An' when they was no meat we ate fowl. An'
when they was no fowl we ate crawdad. An' when they
was no crawdad to be foun', we ate san'.

HI: You ate what?

MOSES (*nodding*):   We ate san'.

HI: You ate sand?!

MOSES: Dass right . . .

PAROLE BOARD ROOM

HI *faces the same three* PAROLE OFFICERS *across the same
table.*

CHAIRMAN: Well Hi, you done served your twenty
munce, and seeing as you never use live ammo, we got
no choice but to return you to society.

SECOND MAN: These doors goan swing wide.

HI: I didn't want to hurt anyone, sir.

SECOND MAN: Hi, we respect that.

CHAIRMAN: But you're just hurtin' yourself with this rambunctious behavior.

HI: I know that, sir.

CHAIRMAN: Okay then.

HIGH SHOT

Of a 7-Eleven parking lot, at night, deserted except for HI's car which sits untended, its engine rumbling.

VO: Now I don't know how you come down on the incarceration question . . .

HI backpedals into frame with a shotgun and a bag of cash.

. . . whether it's for rehabilitation or revenge . . .

He spins and grabs his car-door handle. Locked. He tries the back door. Locked.

. . . But I was beginning to think . . .

As we hear the wail of an approaching siren, HI takes it on the heel and toe.

. . . that revenge is the only argument makes any sense.

FLASH

On HI against the mug-shot wall.

ED: Turn to the right!

Holly Hunter (Ed)

SHERIFF (*os*):   Don't forget his latents, Ed!

CLOSE ON HI'S HAND

We see his right hand being efficiently manipulated by ED*'s two hands: She is rolling each of his inked fingers into the appropriate space on an exemplar sheet.*

HI (*os*):   Hear about the paddy-wagon collided with the see-ment mixer, Ed? . . . Twelve hardened criminals excaped.

ED *titters offscreen.*

ED (*os*):   I heard that one.

She is done rolling off his prints. Her hand lingers on top of his.
    HI*'s other hand enters to rest on top of hers.*

HI (*os*):   Got a new beau?

ED (*os*):   No, Hi, I sure don't.

HI slips a ring off his own finger and slides it onto ED's.

HI (*os*):   Don't worry, I paid for it.

LOW ANGLE   CELL BLOCK CORRIDOR

The surly MOPPING CON has now worked his way up to the foreground.
   HI is being escorted past him to his cell.

VO: They say that absence makes the heart grow fonder, and for once they may be right.

Halfway up the corridor HI points casually at the floor.

HI: You missed a spot.

The MOPPING CON turns to watch him recede.

CON: Grrrr . . .

HIGH ANGLE   CELL

Same high shot with MOSES on the top bunk, HI on the lower.

VO: More and more my thoughts turned to Ed, and I finally felt the pain of imprisonment.

MOSES: An' momma would frow the live crawdad in a pot of boilin' water. Well one day I decided to make my own crawdad . . .

We begin to crane down to tighten on the absently staring HI.

. . . an' I frew it in a pot, forgettin' to put in the water, ya see . . .

MOSES' *voice is mixing down as we lose him from frame.*

. . . and it was like I was makin' popcorn, ya see . . .

VO: The joint is a lonely place after lock-up and lights
out . . .

We are now very close on HI, *staring.*

. . . when the last of the cons has been swept away by
the sandman.

HI'S POV
The underside of the top bunk.
  A sudden flash whitens and fades to leave the image of ED,
*smiling behind her camera, softly supered on the underside of
the bunk.*

BACK TO HI
*He wearily turns his head to profile on the pillow and shuts
his eyes.*

VO: But I couldn't help thinking that a brighter future
lay ahead—a future that was only eight to fourteen
months away.

Eyes closed, he is illuminated by a flash.

PAROLE BOARD ROOM
HI *and the same three officers.*

CHAIRMAN: Got a name for people like you, Hi. That
name is called recidivism.

SECOND MAN: Ree-peat O-fender.

CHAIRMAN: Not a pretty name, is it, Hi?

HI: No sir, it sure ain't. That's one bonehead name. But that ain't me anymore.

CHAIRMAN: You're not just tellin' us what we wanna hear?

HI: No sir, no way.

SECOND MAN: 'Cause we just wanna hear the truth.

HI: Well then I guess I *am* tellin' you what you wanna hear.

CHAIRMAN: Boy, didn't we just tell you not to do that?

HI: Yessir.

CHAIRMAN: Okay then.

TRACKING

Over HI's shoulder as he strides toward a door marked "Processing" and flings it open.
   It is the familiar booking room. ED looks up from her camera, having just snapped a picture of another suspect against the hatched wall.

HI: I'm walkin' in here on my knees, Ed—a free man proposin'.

HI cocks a finger at the suspect.

HI: Howdy Kurt.

ED'S ROOM

As she nervously frets at her white bridal gown in front of a mirror.

VO:　　And so it was.

SHERIFF (*os*):　　Don't forget the boo-kay, Ed!

CLOSE SHOT　ED

Gazing earnestly into the camera. A congregation is seated behind her—the bride's side wearing police blues; the groom's side, Hawaiian shirts.

ED:　　I do.

CLOSE SHOT　HI

Also staring into the camera.

HI:　　You bet I do.

REVERSE

Over their shoulders, the minister.

MINISTER:　　Okay then.

FLASH

On the newlyweds smiling at the camera.

FLASH

On the newlyweds smiling at each other, profile to the camera.

HIGH WIDE SHOT　TRAILER PARK

In the middle of a vast expanse of desert.

VO:　　Ed's pa staked us to a starter home in suburban Tempe . . .

INT MACHINE SHOP

HI is working the drill press, wearing goggles and sweat-stained overalls.

VO: . . . and I got a job drilling holes in sheet metal.

Next to him idly stands BUD, a veteran of the shop, with a grimy face and a pair of goggles pushed up on his forehead.

BUD: So we was doin' paramedical work in affiliation with the state highway system—not actually practicin', y'understand—and me and Bill's patrollin' down Nine Mile—

HI: Bill Roberts?

BUD (*barking*):   No, not that motherscratcher! Bill Parker! Anyway, we're approachin' the wreck, and there's a spherical object a-restin' on the highway . . .

He pauses to blow and pop a bubble with his chewing gum.

. . . And it *don't* look like a piece a the car.

VO: Mostways the job was a lot like prison, except Ed was waitin' at the end of every day . . .

CASHIER'S WINDOW

HI is scowling at his paycheck. Behind the barred window a fat cashier grins.

VO: . . . and a paycheck at the end of every week.

CASHIER: Gummint do take a bite, don't she?

EXT TRAILER

HI sits in a lawn chair in front of the trailer. ED sits on his lap, his arms around her.
   Both are wearing sunglasses, looking at the setting sun. The scene is suffused with a warm yellow light.

VO: These were the happy days, the salad days as they say . . .

As the sun sets, the light is turning from yellow to amber. HI and ED watch, their heads following its slow downward arc.

. . . and Ed felt that having a critter was the next logical step. It was all she thought about.

The amber is turning to a more neutral dusky light as the sun has set. HI and ED continue to stare at the point where it disappeared.

. . . Her point was that there was too much love and beauty for just the two of us . . .

The dusk is slipping away into darkness.

. . . and every day we kept a child out of the world was a day he might later regret having missed.

We are by now holding on pitch black. Crickets chirr. From the darkness:

ED: That was beautiful.

A CALENDAR

ED is crossing off the last day on the calendar before a day circled in red.

VO: So we worked at it on the days we calculated most likely to be fruitful . . .

INT   TRAILER

HI is wearily entering after a long day at work, clutching his lunchpail.

VO: . . . and we worked at it most other days just to be sure.

ED flies into frame and leaps into his arms, covering him with kisses.

TRAILER BEDROOM

In each other's arms, HI and ED roll over on the bed.

VO: Seemed like nothing could stand in our way now . . .

We pan with them rolling and continue off them to the night table, on which sits a framed pair of photographs of HI, probably taken by ED: One shows him full face, the other in profile.

EXT   TRAILER   TWILIGHT

ED sits in a lawn chair knitting a booty. HI stands in Bermuda shorts and an unbuttoned Hawaiian shirt, hosing down the minuscule patch of front lawn.

VO: . . . My lawless years were behind me; our child rearin' years lay ahead.

DUSTY ROAD LEADING UP TO TRAILER   DAY

A squad car, its siren wailing, kicks up dust as it roars into the foreground.

VO: And then the roof caved in.

HI approaches the driver's window as ED leans out sobbing.

ED: Hi, I'm barren.

CLOSE ON HI
Shock and disbelief.

VO: At first I didn't believe it, that this woman who looked as fertile as the Tennessee Valley could not bear children.

DOCTOR'S OFFICE
A doctor is pointing a pencil at various parts of a schematic picture of the female reproductive system, in a book which he holds open on the desk in front of him.

VO: . . . But the doctor explained that her insides were a rocky place where my seed could find no purchase.

REVERSE
On HI and ED seated on the other side of the desk. ED is weeping with grief and shame. HI, one arm draped over her shoulder, is staring dumbstruck at the picture.

VO: Ed was inconsolable.

CLOSE ON A FOLDER
The top sheet is from the Office of the Sheriff, Munroe County. The subject is H. I. McDunnough.

VO: We tried an adoption agency . . .

ADOPTION OFFICE

HI and ED are seated on folding chairs facing an agent's desk. HI wears a sport coat over his Hawaiian shirt. ED is in her dress blues.

HI: It's true I've had a checkered past, but Ed here is an officer of the law twice decorated . . .

THE AGENT

Looking, with a dead pan, from the file to HI.

HI: . . . So we figure it kind of evens out.

His face still deadly neutral, the agent looks back down at the file and unfolds the accordioned rap sheet, revealing it to be a couple feet long.

VO: . . . But biology and the prejudices of others conspired to keep us childless.

INT SQUAD CAR

On ED as she stares vacantly out the passenger window.

VO: Our love for each other was stronger than ever . . .

ON HI

Driving. He looks from ED out to the road.

VO: . . . but I preminisced no return of the salad days.

TRAILER BATHROOM

Over HI's shoulder as he stares listlessly at himself in the mirror, a razor held forgotten in one hand, his face half lathered and half shaved.

VO: The pizzazz had gone out of our lives.

TRAILER BEDROOM

The bedroom is somewhat messy. ED *sits on the edge of the bed, also staring listlessly. Her police uniform is on but not yet buttoned. Her hands lie palm-up in her lap, like two dead fish.*

VO: Ed lost all interest in both criminal justice and housekeeping. Soon after, she tendered her badge.

MACHINE SHOP

Once again HI *works as his sweaty gum-chewing colleague stands idly by.*

VO: Even my job seemed as dry and bitter as a hot prairie wind.

BUD: So here comes Bill a-walkin' down Nine Mile— that's Bill Parker, y'understand—got his sandwich in one hand, the fuckin' head in the other . . .

ON HI DRIVING

Alone in his Chevy. He looks to the side.

VO: I even caught myself drivin' by convenience stores . . .

HIS MOVING POV

7-Eleven.

VO: . . . that weren't on the way home.

TRAILER LIVING ROOM

HI *and* ED *sit listlessly watching TV.*

vo: Then one day the biggest news hit the state since they built the Hoover Dam . . .

ED perks up, reacting to something on TV. HI notices her reaction and also sloughs off his stupor to watch.

. . . The Arizona quints was born.

THE TV

A newscaster silently reading copy. Behind him news footage of five nurses holding infants mortices in.

vo: By "Arizona" quints I mean they was born to a woman named Florence Arizona.

BACK TO HI AND ED

Watching intently. Eyes still locked on the set, ED reaches her hand out to HI. Eyes still locked on the set, HI takes her hand in his.

vo: As you probably guessed, Florence Arizona is the wife of Nathan Arizona. And Nathan Arizona—well hell, you know who he is . . .

THE TV   A LATE-NIGHT LOCAL COMMERCIAL

NATHAN ARIZONA, a stocky middle-aged man in a white polyester suit, is gesturing expansively with his white cowboy hat toward a one-story warehouse store with a football stadium parking lot, chroma-keyed in behind him.

NATHAN ARIZONA (*mixing up on the TV*): So come on down to Unpainted Arizona for the finest selection in fixtures and appointments for your bathroom, bedroom, beaudoir!

VO: . . . The owner of the largest chain of unpainted furniture and bathroom fixture outlets throughout the Southwest.

NATHAN ARIZONA: And if you can find lower prices anywhere my name ain't Nathan Arizona!

BACK TO HI AND ED

As they slowly look from the TV set toward each other.

LINE OF NEWSPAPER VENDING MACHINES

HI lounges near one of the vending machines as a businessman puts in a quarter.

VO: Yep, Florence had been taking fertility pills, and she and Nathan had hit the jackpot.

The businessman takes his newspaper and releases the machine door as he turns to leave.
    HI snags the door before it closes and takes his own five-finger discount copy.
He flips the paper over to look at the headline.

FRONT PAGE OF NEWSPAPER

The banner headline of the Tempe Intelligencer *is:* ARIZONA QUINTS GO HOME! *The subhead: " 'More Than We Can Handle,' Laughs Dad." Next to it is a picture of* NATHAN.

VO: Now y'all who're without sin can cast the first stone . . .

A pull back from the paper shows HI and ED reading it together at home. They look from the paper to each other.
    HI opens to an inside page and we pan a row of pictures—the five tots with their names underneath: HARRY, BARRY, LARRY, GARRY *and* NATHAN JR.

. . . but we thought it was unfair that some should have so many while others should have so few.

BILLBOARD

In the middle of the desert. It reads: "WELCOME TO TEMPE! POPULATION 13,948 . . . PLUS FIVE!"

EXT TRAILER TWILIGHT

We are floating in toward ED who is seated, waiting, in the driver's seat of HI's Chevy. HI enters frame and cinches down a ladder that is tied to the roof of the car. Pieces of red flag flutter at either end of the ladder where it sticks out beyond the car.

VO: With the benefit of hindsight maybe it wasn't such a hot idea . . .

HI gets in the car.

FROM BEHIND THE CHEVY

It starts down the long, winding road leading away from the trailer, kicking up dust.

VO: . . . but at the time, Ed's little plan seemed like the solution to all our problems, and the answer to all our prayers.

*The title of the film burns in: RAISING ARIZONA
    A building chord snaps off in a shock cut to:*

SUBURBAN LIVING ROOM   EVENING

Tableau of a couple at home. NATHAN ARIZONA is on the telephone, his stocking feet up on an ottoman. FLORENCE sits reading Dr. Spock's Baby and Child Care.
    The living room is dominated by a large oil portrait of NATHAN and FLORENCE, gazing out from the wall over the mantelpiece.

NATHAN (*into the phone*):   Eight hundred leaf tables and no chairs?! You can't sell leaf tables and no chairs! Chairs, you got a dinette set! No chairs, you got dick! I ask my wife she got more sense! . . .

A title is supered: THE ARIZONA HOUSEHOLD
From somewhere upstairs we hear an infant start to cry.
FLORENCE *stops reading and looks up at the ceiling.* NATHAN
is oblivious.

NATHAN: . . . Miles, alls I know is I'm away from the office to have me some kids and everything goes straight to heck! I ain't gonna stand for it!

Another title is supered below the first: SEPTEMBER 17, 1985
The baby stops crying and FLORENCE's *attention returns to her book.*

. . . Yeah, and if a frog had wings he wouldn't bump his ass a-hoppin'! I'm sick of your excuses, Miles! It is now . . .

As he throws out his wrist to look at his watch a third title is supered beneath the first two: 8:45 P.M.

. . . 8:45 in the P.M. I'm gonna be down to the store in exactly twelve hours to kick me some butt!

He starts to replace the receiver but brings it back with an afterthought:

. . . Or my name ain't Nathan Arizona!

As he slams the phone into the cradle the titles disappear.
Another baby starts crying. FLORENCE *looks up at the ceiling.*

NATHAN: That sounds like Larry.

NURSERY

Close on the crying baby as HI *bounces it, gently but desperately.*

HI: Shhhh! Shh! Nice baby . . .

He starts to lower it back into the crib. The crib is unpainted with the name of each baby burned Bonanza-style into the headboard: Harry, Barry, Larry, Garry, and Nathan Jr.

Instead of quieting as he is lowered into the crib, the squalling baby only sets off one of his brothers. HI *hurriedly lifts him back out.*

He looks desperately around the room.

The room is wallpapered with nursery rhyme characters. There are toys strewn around. There is one adult-sized easy chair in the corner.

HI *carries the baby over to the chair, stepping on and reacting to the squeal of a squeeze-me toy on the way. He sits the baby deep in the chair and then returns to the crib to deal with the second crying baby.*

He lifts the baby out of the crib and gently bounces it. This baby stops crying.

Another one in the crib starts bawling.

HI *sets the second baby down on the floor and gives it a rattle to keep it pacified. He reaches for the third baby in the crib. Sweat stands out on* HI's *brow. He is desperately chucking the third baby under the chin when we hear a muffled pthump!*

He whirls to look across the darkened room.

The first baby has dropped off the easy chair and is energetically crawling away toward a shadowy corner.

LIVING ROOM

NATHAN *and* FLORENCE *are sitting stock-still, staring at the ceiling. After a moment, another baby starts crying.*

Nicolas Cage

NATHAN: What're they, playing telephone?

They stare at the ceiling.

NURSERY

Loose babies are crawling everywhere.
    HI *is skittering across the room in a half-crouch, a baby tucked under one arm, reaching out with the other as he pursues a crawling baby across the room.*
    He hefts the other baby with his free arm and brings the pair back to the crib.
    He turns to look frantically around the room.
    The other three babies have disappeared.
    There is perfect quiet.
    HI *goes over to the closet door, which is ajar, and swings it open.*
    He reaches under a moving pile of clothes on the floor and pulls out a baby.
    He returns it to the crib and freezes, listening.

The sound of a rattle.
He drops to the floor to look under the crib.

WIDE ANGLE   UNDER CRIB

A baby holding a rattle leers into the camera in the
foreground. Behind him HI, *on his stomach, is reaching in to*
grab at his leg.
    HI *is pulling the baby out, away from the camera, when*
with a plop! a baby drops onto HI's *back from the crib above.*
    HI *twists one arm back to grope for the baby crawling on*
top of him.
    He is straightening up, a baby in each arm, when he reacts
in horror to something he sees across the room.

HIS POV

The hindquarters of a diapered baby are just disappearing
around the corner of the nursery door into the hallway.

LIVING ROOM

FLORENCE *and* NATHAN *are staring at the ceiling. After a*
beat we hear a muffled plop! on the ceiling. A beat later, the
bleat of the squeeze-me toy.

NATHAN: . . . Whyn't you go up and check on 'em?
They sound restless.

UPSTAIRS HALLWAY

The floor-level wide-angle shot shows a baby crawling toward
the camera in the foreground. Behind him, in the background,
just rounding the open door from the nursery, yet another
baby is making a mad dash for freedom.
    HI *emerges from the nursery and, stepping around the*
background baby, trots toward the baby in the foreground. By
the time he reaches it the low-angle cropping shows us only
his feet and calves.

CLOSE ON HI

Perspiring as he tiptoes the last two steps to the baby.

HIS POV

The baby and, beyond it, the stairway down to the main floor. We hear footsteps approaching.

BACK TO HI

He scoops up the baby and hurriedly tiptoes away toward the nursery.

LOW-ANGLE REVERSE

The baby at the nursery door in the foreground; the staircase in the background. As HI *reaches the baby we hear footsteps climbing the stairs.*

HI's free arm comes down into frame to scoop the baby up and out of frame just as:

FLORENCE's head appears, bobbing up as she climbs the stairs.

She approaches the nursery, still clutching the Dr. Spock book.

NURSERY

As FLORENCE *enters from the hallway door.*

We track back into the room, on her, as she approaches the crib. Halfway there she freezes, staring, in shock.

HER POV

All of the babies have been replaced in the crib but not lying down: They are seated in a row, staring back at her, lined up against the far crib railing, like a small but distinguished panel on "Meet the Press."

THROUGH THE WINDSHIELD OF THE CHEVY

ED's point of view of HI *approaching the car. He is shrugging and displaying a pair of manifestly empty hands.*

CLOSE ON ED

Barely able to fight down her anger. Hissing:

ED: What's the matter?!

HI appears at her—the driver's—window.

HI: Sorry honey, it just didn't work out.

He is reaching to open the door but she slaps his hand away from the handle.

ED: What d'you mean it didn't work out?!

HI: They started cryin', then they were all over me . . .

He is trying to open the door, which ED is holding shut with all her might.

. . . It was kinda horrifying—Lemme in, honey.

ED: Course they cried! Babies cry!

HI: I know that now! Come on honey, we better leave—

ED is rolling up the window and locking the door.

ED: You go right back up there and get me a toddler! I need a baby, Hi; they got more'n they can handle!

Muffled, through the closed window, and very forlorn:

HI: Aw honey I—

ED: Don't you come back here without a baby!

NURSERY

FLORENCE is holding one of the babies cradled against her shoulder. She is facing the hallway door; her back is to the crib and window. The baby, peeping out over her shoulder, is facing the window.

CLOSE ON BABY

Looking.

BABY'S POV

Of the window, as HI's head appears in it.

BABY

Looking.

HI

Looking back, he holds a finger to his lips.

BABY

FLORENCE starts bouncing it, patting it on the back.

BABY'S POV

HI and the window bouncing up and down.

LIVING ROOM

NATHAN is leafing through the lingerie ads in the newspaper. We can hear FLORENCE's returning footsteps. Muttering:

NATHAN: Christian Dior my butt . . .

FLORENCE enters.

. . . They pay money for that?

FLORENCE: Yes dear.

NATHAN: How're the kids?

FLORENCE: Fine dear.

NATHAN: Fuckin' kids, I love 'em.

We hear the bleat of the squeeze-me toy. FLORENCE and NATHAN look at the ceiling for a beat, then NATHAN clears his throat and returns to the newspaper.

CHEVY

ED sits anxiously waiting in the driver's seat, peering intently through the windshield. As she catches sight of something she breaks into a broad smile, unlocks the door, and slides over to the passenger seat.

HI is opening the door with one hand, cradling a baby in the other.

ED: Which one ya get?

As he gets into the driver's seat:

HI: I dunno. Nathan Jr., I think.

ED: Gimme here.

He hands her the infant, then hands her the copy of Dr. Spock's Baby and Child Care.

HI: Here's the instructions.

ED: Oh, he's beautiful!

HI nods as he pulls away from the curb.

HI: He's awful damn good. I think I got the best one.

ED is gushing and kissing the baby through the rest of the conversation.

ED: I bet they were all beautiful. All babies are beautiful!

HI: Yeah. This one's awful damn good though.

ED: Don't you cuss around him.

HI: He's fine, he is. I think it's Nathan Jr.

ED: We are doin' the right thing, aren't we Hi?—I mean, they had more'n they could handle.

HI: Well now honey we been over this and over this. There's what's right and there's what's right, and never the twain shall meet.

ED: But you don't think his momma'll be upset? I mean overly?

HI: Well a course she'll be upset, sugar, but she'll get over it. She's got four little babies almost as good as this one. It's like when I was robbin' convenience stores—

ED suddenly bursts out crying.

ED: I love him so much!

HI: I know you do, honey.

ED *(still sobbing)*:   I love him so much!

TRAILER LIVING ROOM

As the lights are thrown on. The room is hung with streamers. A string of cut-out letters reads "Welcome Home Son!"

HI (*os*):   Okay, bring him in!

REVERSE

ED is entering with NATHAN JR.

HI: This is it young Nathan Jr. Just feast your eyes about, old boy!

ED: Don't be so loud around him, Hi.

HI: (*softly*):   Damn, I'm sorry honey.

ED: And don't you cuss around him.

HI: Aw, he don't know a cuss word from shinola.

ED: Well see that he don't.

HI (*jovially*):   He's all right, he is.

He reaches for the child.

. . . Come on over here, Nathan Jr., I'll show you around.

He takes the baby in both hands and holds him out at arm's length, pointing him at the various places of interest. The baby looks google-eyed at each one.

. . . Lookahere, young sportsman. That-there's the kitchen area where Ma and Pa chow down. Over there's the TV, two hours a day maximum, either educational or football so's you don't ruin your appreciation of the finer things. This-here's the divan, for socializin' and relaxin' with the family unit. Yessir, many's the day we sat there and said wouldn't it be nice to have a youngster here to share our thoughts and feelin's—

Impatient with the nonsense:

ED: He's tired, Hi.

HI: Well we'll just sit you right there, boy . . .

He is propping NATHAN JR. *up in the corner of the couch.* HI *sits at the other corner and* ED *sits in a facing chair.*

. . . Just put those dogs up'n take a load off.

HI *beams at* NATHAN JR. ED *smiles at* NATHAN JR. NATHAN JR. *looks from one to the other, deadpan. They seem to be waiting for him to contribute to the conversation.*
Silence.
Suddenly HI *slaps his knee.*

HI: What are you kiddin'?! We got a family here!

ED *is getting up.*

. . . He's a scandal, honey! He's a little outlaw!

As she picks up the baby:

ED: He's a good boy.

HI: He ain't *too* good! You can tell by that twinkle in his eye!

ED: Don't you think we should put him to bed?

HI: Hang on, honey . . .

He is frantically reaching for a Polaroid camera.

. . . Let's us preserve the moment in pictures!

ED: Just one, okay? . . .

She sits down on the couch with NATHAN JR. *as* HI *starts screwing the camera into a tripod.*

. . . I gotta tell ya, I'm a little scared Hi.

Absently, as he sets up the camera:

HI: How come is that, honey?

ED: Well we got a baby, Hi. It's an awful big responsibility.

As he peers through the lens:

HI: Honey, could ya slide over a tad and raise the nipper up?

As she complies:

ED: I mean we never done this before and I'm kinda nervous.

HI: You're doin' real good, sugar.

HI sits on the couch, holding the camera's cable release. He puts his arm around ED *and smiles at the offscreen camera.* ED *nestles her head against* HI's *shoulder.*

ED: I love you, Hi.

HI: We're set to pop here, honey.

ED: You're gonna help, aren't ya?

Through his teeth as he continues to grin at the offscreen camera:

HI: How's that, honey?

ED: Give Nathan Jr. a normal family background, just quiet evenings at home together . . .

We begin to hear distant thunder.

HI: You can count on it, honey.

ED: . . . Everything decent'n normal from here on out.

HI: Uh-huh.

As he squeezes the cable release—FLASH—the image momentarily freezes on HI beaming, NATHAN JR. staring, and ED looking at HI with a little bit of concern.

DARK FIELD   SAME NIGHT

The rolling thunder has built to a thunderclap at the cut, and the flash of the Polaroid match cuts to lightning throwing a momentarily harsh glare on the field.

Rain beats down on the bare patch of ground we are looking at—by now just a patch of mud.

Faraway lightning flickers and we hear the rumble of more thunder approaching, then suddenly:

THWAK—a head pops up out of the mud. It is GALE, the con we saw in group therapy. He bellows as lightning and thunder flash and crack nearby.

His head is covered with mud, although the driving rain is already starting to wash it away.

We are beginning to track in an arc around GALE's *head, who is now struggling, working to get his shoulders and arms up out of the mud. The end of the 180-degree arc and a flash of lightning reveal, way in the distance, the wire-topped walls of a penitentiary.*

Still bellowing, as if in some primal rage, GALE *has gotten his muck-covered arms up out of the earth and is now pushing down to haul up the rest of his body. It comes with much effort, and with the loud sucking-popping sounds of the fiercely clinging mud.*

Finally he is free.

With a great cry, the mud-covered man plunges his right arm straight back down into the earth, all the way up to his shoulder. He gropes intently and then, apparently having grabbed hold of something underground, he starts pulling.

His arm comes slowly back up out of the mud. Clasped in his hand is—a human foot.

Bellowing with effort he continues to pull, liberating the foot . . . leg . . . torso of his companion, and finally his head.

As the rain starts to wash the mud off his companion's head we see that it is his friend EVELLE.

Both are bellowing.

Mud sucks and pops.

Thunder crashes.

INT GAS STATION MEN'S ROOM

At the cut the ear-splitting thunder drops out to quiet. We hear only the muffled patter of rain and the hum of a bare fluorescent.

The two bedraggled escaped cons are standing side by side, combing their hair in the mirror. The men seem absorbed in their task, using hair jelly from a jar that sits on the shelf between them to restore their duck's-ass haircuts.

EVELLE *cracks the bathroom door and looks out into the rain.*

EVELLE: . . . Okay.

GALE: What is it?

EVELLE: Mercury. Looks nice.

EXT   GAS STATION

The two men are trotting out to a Mercury that sits untended at a gas island, a gas hose on automatic stuck in its tank.

As GALE starts up the car EVELLE yanks the hose out and drops it to the ground. GALE is already starting to peel out as EVELLE gets in.

WIDE SHOT   TRAILER LIVING ROOM

Late at night. HI sits asleep on the sofa at the far end of the room, in a pool of lamp light.

We hear faint, distant knocking. As we track in toward HI the knocking becomes louder and more present.

As we approach HI we see that several Polaroids are spread over his gently rising and falling chest.

By the time we tighten on his face the knocking has become quite loud.

VOICE: Open up!

HI starts awake with a grunt.

. . . Open up in air!

He looks up, alarmed.

HIS POV

The front door of the trailer. Someone is pounding insistently.

VOICE: Open up! It's a po-lice!

BACK TO HI

He sits up and tenses. He looks around.
ED stands in her nightgown at the mouth of the hallway, holding NATHAN JR. and squinting at HI. She hisses:

ED: Hi! What's goin' on?

VOICE: Po-lice, son! Open her up!

HI gets to his feet, hurriedly tosses the Polaroids under a cushion of the couch and takes out a gun.

HI: Get in the bedroom.

ED: They ain't gonna take Nathan?!

HI: Well I'd like to see 'em try.

As ED turns back to the bedroom:

VOICE: Open up and maybe we'll letcha plea-bargain.

BEDROOM

As ED enters and shuts the door. She listens hard at the door: HI's footsteps cross the living room, the click of the door opening, silence . . . a burst of raucous male laughter.

HI'S VOICE: . . . Honey! Come on out here! Want you to meet a couple friends of mine!

LIVING ROOM

As ED enters, carrying NATHAN JR. All three men—HI, GALE, and EVELLE—are beaming at her.

HI: Honey, like you to meet Gale and Evelle Snopes, fine a pair as ever broke and entered.

GALE *roars with laughter.*

. . . Boys, this-here's my wife.

GALE: Ma'am.

EVELLE: Miz McDunnough.

ED *smiles politely, then squints at* HI.

ED: Kind of late for visitors, isn't it Hi?

HI: Well yeah honey, but these boys tell me they just got outta the joint. Gotta show a little hospitality.

GALE *is admiring the baby.*

GALE: Well now H.I., looks like you been up to the devil's bidnis!

EVELLE: That a him or a her?

ED: It's a little boy.

GALE: Got a name, does he?

HI *and* ED *look at each other uncomfortably.* HI *clears his throat.*

HI: Well so far we just been using Junior.

ED: We call him Junior.

EVELLE: Say, that's good—J.R., just like on the Teevee.

GALE *is staring at the streamers and decorations. Reading aloud:*

GALE: "Welcome . . . Home . . . Son." Where's he been?

HI and ED respond simultaneously:

HI: Tulsa.

ED: Phoenix.

HI: He was, uh . . . he was visiting his grandparents.

ED: They're separated.

GALE: Was that yer folks ma'am?

ED: No, I'm afraid not.

GALE: I thought yer folks was dead, H.I.?

HI (*very uncomfortably*):   Well we thought Junior should see their final resting place—Whyn't you boys have a seat?

As the two men move toward the couch ED hesitantly pipes up:

ED: Hi, it's two in the morning . . .

She wrinkles her nose.

. . . What's that smell?

Apologetically:

GALE: We don't always smell like this, Miz McDunnough. I was just explainin' to yer better half here that when we were tunnelin' out we hit the main sewer—dumb luck, that—and just followed that to—

ED: You mean you *busted* out of jail?!

GALE: Waaaal . . .

EVELLE: We released ourselves on our own recognizance.

GALE: What Evelle means to say is, we felt the institution no longer had anything to offer us . . .

He is looking at the baby.

. . . My Lord he's cute.

EVELLE: He's a little outlaw, you can see that.

ED: Now listen, you folks can't stay here!

GALE, EVELLE, and HI look up at ED, dumbstruck. After a beat:

EVELLE: . . . Ma'am?

ED: You just can't stay! I appreciate your bein' friends of Hi and all, but this is a decent family now . . .

She looks at HI.

. . . I mean we got a toddler here!

GALE leans in close to HI, a look of sincere concern on his face, and says under his breath:

GALE: Say, who wears the pants round here H.I.?

HI: Now honey—

ED: Don't you honey me. Now you boys can set a
while and catch up, and then you'll be on your way.

*There is an awkward silence as she leaves and slams the
bedroom door.*
        *GALE is carefully studying his thumbnail; EVELLE stares
fixedly at the ceiling. Still looking at his thumb:*

GALE: Gotcha on a awful short leash, don't she H.I.?

BEDROOM

*Sometime later, as HI tiptoes in. ED lies in bed facing the
wall; we see only the back of her head. HI sits gingerly on the
edge of the bed and, smiling, sticks a finger through the bars
of the crib to play with the baby.*
        *The sound of the TV set in the living room filters faintly
in.*

ED: They still here?

*HI is momentarily startled, then goes on playing with the
baby.*

HI: Yeah, they're just gonna stay a day or two. It's
raining out honey, they got nowhere to go.

*ED finally turns to face him. We hear the two men laugh
raucously in the living room.*

ED: They're fugitives, Hi . . .

HI turns to face her.

. . . How're we gonna start a new life with them
around?

HI: Well now honey you gotta have a little charity. Ya know, in Arab lands they'd set out a plate—

ED: Promise just a day or two.

HI: Tonight and tomorrow, tops.

EXTREME HIGH ANGLE

Looking straight down at HI, asleep in bed. It is later: filtering softly in from the other room is the end of the "Star Spangled Banner" on TV. We are craning down.

VO: That night I had a dream . . .

FLASH CUT

For a brief moment we see a wall of flames and hear it roar.

BACK TO HI

Still craning down.

VO: . . . I'd drifted off thinkin' about happiness, birth, and new life . . .

FLASH CUT

Wall of flames. Deafening roar.

BACK TO HI

Craning down. The faint National Anthem ends: we hear the WEEEEEEEE of a test pattern.

VO: . . . but now I was haunted by a vision of—

WALL OF FLAMES

Roaring. At the cut: WHOOOOOSH! a huge low-rider motorcycle bursts through the flames, its engine roaring even

*louder than the fire. Its driver is a huge leather-clad hellion.
The chains worn by the* BIKER *clank ominously as he rides.*

VO: He was horrible . . .

The BIKER *roars out of frame.*

LOW-ANGLE REVERSE

As the BIKER *roars into frame, his rear tire laying down a
wake of fire.*

VO: . . . a lone biker of the apocalypse . . .

TRACKING ON BIKER

As he roars along a ribbon of desert highway.

VO: . . . a man with all the powers of hell at his
command.

The BIKER *reaches for his bullwhip.*

. . . He could turn the day into night . . .

The BIKER *cracks the whip and, at the crack:
   The sky behind him turns instantly to black. Bolts of
lightning crackle across it as thunder roars.*

ANOTHER DESERT SCENE   DAY

Tracking with and also in on the BIKER *from behind as he
roars along a strip of highway. He is reaching for the two
sawed-off shotguns which are strapped crisscross across his
back.*

VO: . . . and laid to waste everything in his path.

REVERSE TRACK ON BIKER

Pulling the BIKER *from a distance as he levels the two shotguns. The tracking camera pulls back further to reveal a running jack-rabbit keeping pace with us in the foreground.*

VO: He was especially hard on the little things . . .

CRACK—as the first shotgun spurts orange the foreground rabbit keels over. The BIKER *slues the other gun around.*

LOCKED-DOWN WIDE SHOT

On a rock in the foreground, a desert lizard suns himself. The BIKER *is approaching in the distant background.*

VO: . . . the helpless and the gentle creatures.

CRACK—from afar, the foreground lizard is blown away.

LOCKED-DOWN LOW-ANGLE WIDE SHOT

Of the empty desert road stretching away. In the foreground a lone desert flower blooms. The BIKER *roars into frame.*

VO: He left a scorched earth in his wake, befouling even the sweet desert breeze that whipped across his brow.

As the BIKER *roars away, the foreground flower bends with his draft and then bursts into flame.*

TRACKING ON BIKER

From in front. He twirls the shotguns in either hand and reaches back to plunge them over his shoulders into their holsters.

VO: I didn't know where he came from or why . . .

*We are moving in on his chest, where two crisscrossed
bandoliers carry two rows of hand grenades, their silver pins
glinting in the sun. We follow the line of one of the bandoliers
up to his right shoulder which bears the tattoo: "Mama
Didn't Love Me."*

. . . I didn't know if he was dream or vision . . .

REVERSE TRACK ON BIKER

*From behind, booming down as we track. We are approaching
the crest of a rise.*

VO: But I feared that I myself had unleashed him . . .

HIGH SHOT

Of the BIKER approaching, craning down as he draws near.

VO: . . . for he was The Fury That Would Be . . .

*With the crane down we momentarily lose him from view
over the rise; then suddenly—ROAR—he tops the rise and,
wheels spinning, is airborn.*

REVERSE

*As he crashes back down to earth in the foreground and roars
away. Only now we are no longer in the desert: We are
looking down a twilit street at the end of which is the Arizona
house.*

VO: . . . as soon as Florence Arizona found her little
Nathan gone.

*The roar of his engine and clank of his chains recede as the
BIKER gradually dissolves into thin air.*
    *We are left looking at the empty street and the faraway
Arizona house.*
    The receding roar has left behind eerily beautiful singing, a

*woman singing a lullaby. Faintly, behind the singing, there
is also a droning high-pitched noise.*

*The camera starts floating forward very close to the
ground, moving slowly toward the Arizona house. The high-
pitched drone is becoming less faint under the singing.*

*The camera is accelerating. The drone is growing louder—
we can now tell that it is a human scream.*

*As we approach the Arizona house we can see that a ladder
is propped up to a second-story window.*

*We are moving quite fast now. The scream all but buries
the singing.*

*We are rushing toward the house, toward the base of the
ladder, the sustained scream drawing us on.*

*We hurtle toward and then straight up the ladder with
no abatement of speed, sucked forward by the deafening
scream.*

*We reach the top and hurtle—THWAP!—through the
white curtains of the open second-story window into the
nursery to reveal* FLORENCE ARIZONA, *her back to us,
screaming over the crib.*

We are rocketing toward her.

*She is turning to us, hands pressed to her ears, mouth
stretched wide in an ear-splitting shriek and we are rushing
into an extreme close-up of her gaping mouth and her wildly
vibrating epiglottis and we*

CUT TO:

EXTREME CLOSE SHOT   HI'S EYES

As they snap open.

*The screaming snaps off at the cut. The singing that the
building scream covered, however, is now audible again.*

Perspiration beads HI's *forehead. He looks down toward the
foot of the bed.*

THE BEDROOM

It is now morning. ED *walks back and forth, gently bouncing the baby as she walks. She is singing it a lullaby.*

Faintly, from the next room, we can hear GALE *and* EVELLE *snoring away like buzz saws.*

HI (*groggily*):   He all right?

ED: He's all right. He was just havin' a nightmare.

HI is getting out of bed.

HI: Yeah, well . . .

He crosses to the bedroom window and cracks the venetian blind. Orange light filters in.

HIS POV

Beyond a clothes line and a septic tank, a huge orange ball of sun is rising. We can almost hear the roar of its burning surface.

BACK TO HI

Looking.

HI: . . . Sometimes it's a hard world for little things.

HIS POV

The orange sun, rumbling, perceptibly rising.

ARIZONA HOME   FRONT FOYER

At the cut the rumble of the sun is snapped off by the high-pitched ba-WEEEEeeee . . . of a strobe going off as a flash picture is taken: We are looking over NATHAN SR.*'s shoulder as he stands at his open front door, facing a battery of press people who stand out on the porch.*

*An obie light over a local TV news camera glares in at us;
various flashbulbs pop.*

NATHAN: —No, the missus and the rest of the kids've
left town to I ain't sayin' where. They'll be back here
when we're a nuclear fam'ly again.

VOICE: Mr. Arizona, which tot was abducted?

NATHAN: Nathan Jr., I think.

VOICE: Do you have anything to say to the kidnappers?

NATHAN: Yeah: Watch yer butt.

VOICE: Sir, it's been rumored that your son was
abducted by UFOs. Would you care to comment?

NATHAN *(sadly)*:   Now don't print that, son. If his
mama reads that she's just gonna lose all hope.

*A POLICEMAN from inside the house is taking NATHAN by the
elbow.*

POLICEMAN: We really have to ask you some more
questions, sir . . .

*As NATHAN allows himself to be led back into the house he
calls back over his shoulder:*

NATHAN: But remember, it's still business as usual at
Unpainted Arizona, and if you can find lower prices
anywhere my name still ain't Nathan Arizona!

*We are following the two, hand-held, as the POLICEMAN leads
NATHAN toward the living room.*

LIVING ROOM

The room is filled with policemen milling about in several different uniforms: local police, state troopers, plainclothes detectives.

The original POLICEMAN *is leading* NATHAN *to a table where a white-smocked technician is preparing inkpad and exemplar sheets.*

The dialogue is urgent, rapid-fire and overlapping.

POLICEMAN: Mr. Byrum here can take your exemplars while you talk.

MR. BYRUM *has taken* NATHAN's *right hand and is rolling its fingers onto the inkpad.*

BYRUM: Just let your hand relax; I'll do the work.

NATHAN *jerks his hand away.*

NATHAN: What is this?! I didn't steal the damn kid!

Two men in conservative suits are approaching.

POLICEMAN: Sir, these men are from the FBI—

NATHAN (*bewildered*):   Are you boys crazy?! Alls I know is I wake up this morning with my wife screaming—

BYRUM (*patiently*):   We just need to distinguish your prints from the perpetrators', if they left any.

Giving his hand back:

NATHAN: Course! *I* know that!

FBI 1:   Sir, we have an indication you were born Nathan Huffhines; is this correct?

NATHAN: Yeah, I changed m'name; what of it?

FBI 2:   Could you give us an indication why?

NATHAN: Yeah, would you buy furniture at a store called Unpainted Huffhines?

FBI 1:   All right, I'll get to the point—

UNIFORMED COP: Was the child wearing anything when he was abducted?

NATHAN: No one sleeps nekkid in this house, boy! He was wear—

FBI 1:   I'm asking the questions here, officer.

COP: If we're gonna put out an APB we need a description of the—

NATHAN: He was wearin' his—

FBI 2:   It's just that we're better trained to intervene in crisis situations (*to* NATHAN). What was he wearing?

NATHAN: A dinner jacket! Wuddya think, he was wearing his damn jammies!

FBI 2 (*to* COP):   The child was wearing his jammies. Are you happy?

FBI 1:   Do you have any disgruntled employees?

NATHAN: Hell, they're all disgruntled! I ain't runnin' a damn daisy farm!

COP: What did the pyjamas—

NATHAN: My motto is do it my way or watch your butt!

COP: What did the pyjamas—

FBI 1:   So you think it might have been an employee?

NATHAN: Don't make me laugh. Without my say-so they don't piss with their pants on fire.

COP: What did the pyjamas look like?

FBI 1 (*pained*):   Officer—

NATHAN (*bellowing*):   I dunno, they were jammies! They had Yodas'n shit on 'em!

BELLOWING VOICE OFFSCREEN: Would ya mind, I'm trying to set up a Command Post here!

NATHAN bellows back:

NATHAN: Get your feet off m'damn coffee table!

Also raising his voice at the offscreen bellower:

FBI 1:   Ron, you're upsetting the victim.

NATHAN is getting worked up.

NATHAN: Damnit, are you boys gonna go chase down your leads or are you gonna sit drinkin' coffee in the one house in the state where I know my boy ain't at?!

FBI 2:   Sir, there aren't any "leads" yet, aside from this coat—

NATHAN: Gimme that!

He grabs the overcoat being displayed by FBI 2.

NATHAN: That's a five-hundred-dollar camel's hair—

BYRUM: Sir, you might want to wash your hands at this point.

NATHAN realizes that he's gotten ink from his fingerprinting all over the coat.

NATHAN: Well goddamnit!

He is rising to his feet and hurling the coat to the floor.

. . . No leads?!

He furiously kicks the coat.

. . . Everyone leaves microbes'n whatnot!

Throughout the speech NATHAN stalks the room, working himself into a frenzy, furiously putting coffee cups onto coasters, generally cleaning up, hectoring the police, and swiping their feet off his furniture.

. . . Hell, that's your forte, trackin' down them microbes left by criminals'n commies'n shit! That's yer whole damn raison d'être! No leads?! I want Nathan Jr. back, or whichever the hell one they took! He's out there *some*where! Somethin' *leads* to him! And anyone can find him knows the difference between a lead and a hole in the ground!!

A HOLE IN THE GROUND   DAY

Specifically, it is the hole in the muddy patch of earth that GALE and EVELLE climbed out of. We hear only the squish-

suck of many feet walking around in the mud offscreen.

We are pulling back to reveal the feet—the shiny black patent leather shoes and blue pants cuffs—becoming quickly spattered—of several policemen milling about the hole. German shepherds sniff around also.

With a roar, motorcycle wheels enter frame. The bike's jackbooted rider casually tools around the hole once; police step back and dogs skitter away to give him room.

He backs toward the camera and stops, standing astride the bike. The burning stub of a cheroot is dropped into frame; it hisses angrily and dies in the mud. We start to crane up.

The whipcracking BIKER cue mixes up. The BIKER's motorcycle idles with a deep rumble, like the roar of fire on the sun.

We are now framed looking over the BIKER's shoulder. The policemen's attitude to him seems to be deferential. One cop in front of him is pointing a direction. The BIKER is shaking his head; he doesn't think they went that way.

Suddenly, with a loud whipcrack effect, the BIKER's head snaps to profile. He is staring across the field, stock-still, having heard, smelled or sensed something.

The dogs milling around the hole also react, snapping to attention, a split second after the BIKER.

THEIR POV

A jackrabbit is bounding away at the far end of the field.

THE DOGS

After a moment, their attention returns to the hole.

THE BIKER

His attention also returns to the matter at hand. He squints, concentrating. His bike rumbles. Gradually his face sets in a specific direction.

We pan down to the tattoo on his shoulder: "Mama Didn't Love Me." His shoulder flexes once or twice as he revs the *throttle; then he puts the bike in gear and it roars out of frame.*

TRAILER KITCHEN   CLOSE ON GALE AND EVELLE

They are both intently munching cornflakes, staring at something offscreen. After a beat:

EVELLE: . . . Awful good cereal flakes, Miz McDunnough.

THEIR POV

ED is sitting in the living room, bottle-feeding NATHAN JR. She is surrounded by the rumpled sheets and blankets used by the house guests. She does not respond to the ice-breaker.

GALE puts his spoon down and picks up a cigarette which has been smoking in the ashtray next to him. There is a bead of milk dribbling down his chin.

He takes a contemplative puff, studying ED.

William Forsythe (Evelle) and John Goodman (Gale)

GALE: . . . Whyncha breast feed him? You 'pear to be capable.

ED: Mind your own bidnis.

Through a mouthful of cornflakes:

EVELLE: Ya don't breast feed him, he'll hate you for it later. That's why we wound up in prison.

GALE blows out smoke and picks up his spoon to start back in on his cornflakes.

GALE: Anyway, that's what Doc Schwartz tells us.

HI is walking in, yawning.

HI: Boys.

EVELLE: Mornin', H.I.

Sharply, as HI sits and starts to pour cornflakes into a bowl:

ED: . . . Hi.

HI holds the cornflakes box arrested in mid-air. He looks at ED, who is motioning to GALE and EVELLE with her eyes.

HI: Oh yeah . . . Say boys, you wouldn't mind makin' yourself scarce for a couple hours this afternoon?

ED: We're havin' some *decent* friends over.

GALE and EVELLE are looking dumbly from ED to HI.

HI: Heh-heh . . . What Ed means to say is, seein' as you two boys are wanted, it wouldn't exactly do to have folks seein' you here—I mean for your own protection.

GALE: Sure H.I.

EVELLE: Anything you say.

More relaxed now, to ED:

HI: Matter of fact honey, maybe I'll skip this little get-together myself, Glen won't mind, and I'll just duck out with the boys, knock back a couple of—uh, Co'Colas—

GALE: Sure H.I.

EVELLE: We'd love to have ya.

CLOSE ON ED
Looking pleadingly at HI.

BACK TO HI
Feeling the look, he goes back to his cornflakes.

HI: . . . Well . . . maybe that ain't such a hot idea either.

GALE *leans back to blow smoke at the ceiling.*

GALE (*bitterly*):   So many social engagements. So little time.

WIDE SHOT   GAS STATION BATHROOM
It is the bathroom where we earlier saw GALE *and* EVELLE *combing their hair, now empty.*
    We are looking toward the door. The bathroom is quiet except for the dripping sink, and the faint rumble of an approaching motorcycle. It grows louder, then begins to recede as the bike shoots by the station.
    Suddenly we hear the screech of the bike's brakes.

EXT THE STATION

We are on the road outside the gas station as the motorcycle screeches to a halt in the foreground. The low wide shot crops the BIKER *at his shins. In the background behind him is the gas station.*

The BIKER *pauses for a moment, thinking or feeling.*

BACK TO INT BATHROOM

We hear the rumble of the bike approaching, very loud.

CRASH—the bathroom door flies open as the BIKER *bursts in astride his hog, bright daylight streaming in with him to throw him into imposing silhouette. The shafts of light pouring in are defined by motes of dust dancing in the air.*

HIS POV

Fast track in on the jar of hair jelly sitting on the shelf under the mirror.

BACK TO BIKER

An extreme close shot shows his nostrils dilating as we hear him sniff.

He revs the rumbling bike, stealing thunder from a far mountain.

FRONT STOOP OF TRAILER

HI, *with* ED *standing by, is just opening the door to a young couple.* GLEN *is a short stocky blond man in his early thirties, wearing Bermuda shorts.* DOT *is wearing slacks, heels, and a scarf over her hair.*

HI: Glen, Dot—

As the door opens, DOT *hops up the stoop shrieking.*

DOT: Where's at baby? Where's he at?

From behind, GLEN *gives her an energetic THWOK on the ass.*

GLEN: Go find him honey!

DOT *spins and smacks* GLEN *across the face with her purse. Through clenched teeth:*

DOT: Cut it out, Glen!

He reels under the blow.

ED (*quietly*):   He's asleep right now.

DOT *shrieks again, but this time muffles it with her own hand. She tiptoes into the trailer, hand to her mouth.* GLEN, *rubbing his cheek, seems angry at himself.*

GLEN: Shit, I hope we didn't wake it!

DOT: Can I just sneak a peek-a-loo?

GLEN, *at the top of the stoop, turns out to the yard.*

GLEN: Come on kids . . .

WIDE SHOT   GLEN AND DOT'S KIDS

A scad of children, ranging in age from two to seven, are crawling over HI's *car. One is beating on it with a large stick, another sits on the hood pulling back one of the windshield wipers, etc.*

GLEN: . . . Get away from Mr. McDunnough's car.

TRAILER BEDROOM

As ED *and* DOT *enter,* ED *beaming as they go to the crib.*

DOT: What's his name?

ED: Uh . . . Hi Jr. Till we think of a better one.

DOT: Whyncha call him Jason? I love Biblical names. If I had another little boy I'd name him Jason or Caleb or Tab. Oh!—

She puts her hand to her forehead, reacting to the baby as if she is about to faint.

. . . He's an angel!

She hides her face in her hands and looks away as if blinded, then sneaks a look around her hands.

Frances McDormand (Dot) and Holly Hunter

. . . He's an angel straight from heaven! Now honey I had all my kids the hard way so you gotta tell me where you got this angel. Did he fly straight down from heaven?

ED: Well—

DOT: You gonna send him to Arizona State?

TRAILER LIVING ROOM/KITCHEN

The weaving knee-level tracking shot is following a six-year-old boy in shorts and a dirty T-shirt as he tramps around the trailer, brandishing a big stick. He strikes the walls, furniture, various other objects with his stick, hollering "Bam! Bam-Bam!" with each blow.

The track weaves off him and onto HI, *who is bending down to pull a couple of beers from the refrigerator. He raises his voice to make himself heard over the din of all the children boiling around the room:*

HI: Need a beer, Glen?

GLEN: Does the Pope wear a funny hat?

HI considers this.

HI: . . . Well yeah, Glen, I guess it is kinda funny.

GLEN: Say, that reminds me! How many Pollacks it take to screw up a lightbulb?

HI: I don't know Glen, one?

HI looks down.

One of GLEN's *children, in a cowboy hat, is squirting a squirt gun into his crotch area.*

GLEN: Nope, it takes three!

He starts laughing, then catches himself.

. . . Wait a minute, I told it wrong. Here, I'm startin' over: How come it takes three Pollacks to screw up a lightbulb?

HI: I don't know, Glen.

GLEN: Cause they're so durn stupid!

He laughs; HI doesn't react.

. . . Shit man, loosen up! Don't ya get it?

HI looks over at the TV, which the bam-shouting six-year-old is banging with his stick.

HI: No Glen, I sure don't.

GLEN: Shit man, think about it! I guess it's what they call a Way Homer.

HI: Why's that?

GLEN: Cause you only get it on the Way Home.

HI: I'm already home, Glen.

The kid in the cowboy hat is reaching up to slap HI on the ass.

KID: You wetchaseff! Mr. McDunnough wet hisseff, Daddy!

GLEN: Say, that reminds me! How'd you get that kid s'darned fast? Me'n Dottie went in to adopt on account of something went wrong with m'semen, and they told us five years' wait for a healthy white baby! I said healthy white baby! Five years! Okay, what else you got? Said, two Koreans and one Negro born with the heart outside . . .

  He takes a sip of beer.

  . . . Yeah, it's a crazy world.

HI: Someone oughta sell tickets.

GLEN: Sure, I'd buy one.

  HI is looking at another child who is just finishing off the T in
  FART in crayon on the wall.
  GLEN chuckles, looking at his errant child.

  . . . That Buford's a sly one. Already knows his ABCs. But I'm sayin', how'd ya get the kid?

HI: Well this whole thing is just who knows who and favoritism. Ed has a friend at one of the agencies.

GLEN: Well maybe she can do something for me'n Dot. See there's something wrong with m'semen. Say, that reminds me! What you gonna call him?

HI: Uh, Ed—Ed Jr.

GLEN: Thought you said he was a boy.

HI: Well, as in Edward. Just like that name.

GLEN (*not really interested*): Yeah, it's a good one . . .
Course I don't really need another kid, but Dottie says
these-here are gettin' too big to cuddle. Say, that reminds
me!—

There is the sound of shattering glass. GLEN *looks around.*

GLEN: Mind ya don't cutchaseff, Mordecai . . .

EXT PICNIC GROUNDS

DOT *faces* HI *and* ED *across a picnic table covered with grilled
hamburgers, rolls, green jello mold, cooler, etc.*
    *One of the younger children sits in the middle of the table,
occasionally taking a fistful of jello and flinging it at* HI. *The
two women don't seem to notice.*

DOT: —and then there's diphtheria-tetanus, what they
call dip-tet. You gotta get him dip-tet boosters yearly or
else he'll get lockjaw and night vision. Then there's the
smallpox vaccine, chicken pox and measles, and if your
kid's like ours you gotta take all those shots first to get
him to take 'em. Who's your pediatrician, anyway?

ED: We ain't exactly fixed on one yet. Have we Hi?

HI *sits stock-still with a stony face.*

. . . No, I guess we don't have one yet.

DOT *shrieks.*

DOT: Well you just gotta have one! You just gotta have
one this instant!

ED: Yeah, what if the baby gets sick, honey?

DOT: Hell, even if he don't get sick he's gotta have his dip-tet!

ED: He's gotta have his dip-tet, honey.

HI shrugs, then flinches as a piece of jello hits his shoulder.

HI: . . . Uh-huh.

DOT: You started his bank accounts?

ED: Have we done that honey? We gotta do that honey. What's that for, Dot?

DOT: That-there's for his orthodonture and his college. You soak his thumb in iodine you might get by without the orthodonture, but it won't knock any off the college.

HI sits stoically. DOT is looking offscreen:

. . . Reilly, take that diaper off your head and put it back on your sister! . . . Anyway, you probably got the life insurance all squared away.

ED: You done that yet honey?

DOT: You gotta do that, Hi! Ed here's got her hands full with that little angel!

HI (*dully*):   Yes ma'am.

DOT: What would Ed and the angel do if a truck came along and splattered your brains all over the interstate? Where would you be then?

ED: Yeah honey, what if you get run over?

DOT: Or you got carried off by a twister?

LAKESIDE PATH

We are tracking on HI *and* GLEN *as they walk side by side.*
GLEN *is sopping wet, wearing only swimming suit and wing-
tipped shoes. His body is ghostly pale except for a V-area at
his neck and his arms below the short-sleeve line, which are a
bright angry red.*

GLEN: Hear about the person of the Polish persuasion
he walks into a bar holdin' a pile of shit in his hands,
says "Look what I almost stepped in."

GLEN bursts out laughing; HI *walks on in silence.*

HI: . . . Yeah, that's funny all right . . .

GLEN: Ya damn right it's funny! Shit man, what's the
matter?

HI: I dunno . . . maybe it's wife, kids, family life . . . I
mean are you, uh, satisfied Glen? Don't y'ever feel
suffocated? Like, like there's somethin' big pressin'
down . . .

GLEN (*solemnly*):   Eeeeeyep . . . I *do* know the feelin'.

HI shakes his head.

HI: I dunno—

GLEN: And I *told* Dottie to lose some weight but she
don't wanna listen!

He roars with laughter and slaps HI *heartily on the back. As
he chuckles sympathetically:*

. . . No man, I know what you mean. You got all kinds a responsibilities now. You're married, ya got a kid, looks like your whole life's set down and where's the excitement?

HI: Yeah Glen, I guess that's it.

GLEN: Okay! That's the disease, but there is a cure.

HI: Yeah?

GLEN: Sure; Doctor Glen is tellin' ya you can heal thyself.

HI: What do I gotta do?

GLEN: Well you just gotta broaden your mind a little bit. I mean say I asked you, what do you think about Dot?

HI (*puzzled*):   Fine woman you got there.

GLEN is eyeing him shrewdly.

GLEN: Okay. Now it might not look like it, but lemme tell you something: She's a hellcat.

HI: That right?

GLEN: T-I-G-E-R.

HI: But what's that got to do with—

GLEN: Don't rush me!

He stops walking. HI stops also, looking at GLEN, still puzzled. GLEN lays a companionable hand on his shoulder.

. . . Now the thing about Dot is, she thinks—and she's
told me this—

*He looks around as if to make sure they are not being
overheard. His tone is confidential.*

. . . she thinks . . . you're cute.

HI looks suspiciously at GLEN's hand on his shoulder.

HI: . . . Yeah. . . ?

GLEN nods energetically:

GLEN: I'm crappin' you negative! And *I* could say the
same about Ed!

Through tightly clenched teeth:

HI: What're you talkin' about, Glen?

GLEN: What'm I talkin' about?! I'm talkin' about sex,
boy! What the hell're *you* talkin' about?! You know,
"l'amour"?! I'm talkin' me'n Dot are Swingers! As in "to
Swing"! Wife-swappin'! What they call nowadays Open
Marriage!

*Beaming, he takes his hand off HI's shoulder and spreads his
arms.*

GLEN: I'm talkin' about the Sex Revolution! I'm talkin'
about—

*THWAK—HI's fist swings into frame to connect solidly with
GLEN's jaw.*
   *GLEN's feet leave the ground. He flies back and lands in a
heap.*

LOW-ANGLE REVERSE

GLEN *in the foreground, groggily rubbing his jaw;* HI *approaching menacingly.*

HI: Keep your goddamned hands off my wife!

GLEN: Shit man!

He is scrambling to his feet.

. . . I was only tryin' to help!

HI: Keep your goddamned hands off my wife!

With HI *still advancing,* GLEN *starts to run.*

TRACKING ON GLEN

With HI *pursuing in the background.*
    GLEN *is looking back over his shoulder to shout at* HI *as he runs.*

GLEN: You're crazy! I feel pity for you, man! You—

*CRASH!—*GLEN *runs smack into a tree and drops like a sack of cement.*

INT CAR NIGHT

HI *is driving, his jaw rigidly set, his temple throbbing.*
NATHAN JR. *sits in a safety seat between him and* ED.

ED: We finally go out with some decent people and you break his nose. That ain't too funny, Hi.

HI (*stolidly*):   His kids seemed to think it was funny.

ED: Well they're just kids, you're a grown man with responsibilities. Whatever possessed you?

HI: He was provokin' me when I popped him.

ED: How'd he do that?

HI: . . . Never mind.

ED: But Hi, he's your foreman, he's just gonna fire you now.

HI: I expect he will.

ED: And where does that leave me and Nathan Jr.?

HI: With a man for a husband.

He is pulling into a convenience store parking lot.

ED: That ain't no answer.

HI: Honey, that's the only answer.

He puts the car in park but leaves it running.

. . . Nathan needs some Huggies. I'll be out directly.

As he gets out of the car:

. . . Mind you stay strapped in.

INT STORE
CLOSE SHOT L'EGGS RACK

A hand enters to take a package of panty hose from the standing rack.

CLOSE SHOT   HUGGIES

A hand enters to take a big carton of disposable diapers from the shelf.

CLOSE UP   CASHIER

A pimply-faced lad with a paper 7-Eleven cap on his head. He is looking up from a dirty magazine, reacting in horror to something approaching.

HIS POV

HI is approaching the check-out island with a gun in one hand, the carton of Huggies tucked under the other. The L'Eggs stocking is pulled over his head to distort his features.

HI: I'll be taking these Huggies and whatever cash you got.

CLOSE SHOT   CASHIER'S HAND

As he presses a silent alarm under the lip of his counter.

EXT   CAR

ED is reading to NATHAN JR. from a large picture book.

ED: " 'Not by the hair of my chinny-chin-chin.' 'Then I'll huff and I'll puff . . .' "

She pauses for a moment, listening. We can barely hear a distant siren. She resumes absently, but her voice trails off:

" '. . . and I'll blow your house in . . .' "

We can definitely hear the WHOO-WHOO of the siren now, and it is definitely approaching. ED hooks an arm around the seat and looks behind the car, then looks forward.

HER POV

Indistinctly visible through the semi-reflective glass are two figures at the check-out island. One is pointing something at the other.

BACK TO ED

As the siren is growing louder. Under her breath:

ED: That son of a bitch.

She unstraps herself and gets out of the car.

INT STORE

Two-shot of HI and the CASHIER, who is stuffing bills into a grocery bag. Beyond them we can see ED, outside, circling the front of the car.
    Her shout is muffled through the glass:

ED: You son of a bitch!

With this HI notices her. He turns to the CASHIER.

HI: Better hurry it up. I'm in dutch with the wife.

But ED is already getting into the driver's seat of the car.

BACK TO ED

As she slams the car door shut. The siren is quite loud now.

ED: That son of a bitch. Hang on, pumpkin.

The car squeals out of the lot.

WIDE SHOT   THE STREET

The squad car tops a rise to bounce into view, its siren wailing.

BACK TO THE STORE

HI bursts out the door, still wearing the stocking. The carton of Huggies is still tucked under one arm.
Bellowing hopefully after his departing car:

HI: Honey!

We hear the SMACK-CRACK of a gunshot and glass impact, but the approaching squad car is still too far down the block to have been the source.
HI looks around the parking lot, bewildered.
The wailing siren is becoming painfully loud.
HI looks behind him at the plate-glass front of the store, where a bullet pock mars the glass.

HIS POV

Through the glass we see the pimply young CASHIER with the paper 7-Eleven cap pop up from behind the counter to sight down his huge .44 Magnum for another shot. The gun is so big he uses both hands to heft it.
SMACK-CRACK—the bullet kisses another hole in the glass.
HI is off and running.
The squad car is screeching into the lot. An officer tumbles out of the passenger side before the car is fully stopped. He rolls on the pavement, then hurriedly rights himself and takes up a half-kneeling shooting stance.
At the same time the little CASHIER is emerging from the 7-Eleven with his gun.
The two bang away at HI's retreating figure—the POLICEMAN's revolver popping, the CASHIER's Magnum booming.
We hear the POLICEMAN who is still in the car drawling over its loudspeaker:

SPEAKER: Halt. It's a police warning, son. Put those groceries down and turn yourself in.

TRACKING ON HI

Legs pumping, panty hose still over his head, its unused leg streaming behind him like an aviator's scarf. The gun is tucked into his belt; the Huggies are tucked securely under his arm.

Behind him we can see the OFFICER *and the* CASHIER *squeeze off another couple shots, and then the policeman piles back into the squad car.*

ED'S CAR

Driving. She hears distant gunshots.

ED: That son of a bitch . . . Hold on, Nathan. We're gonna go pick up Daddy.

She hangs a vicious U-turn.

TRACKING ON HI

Huffing and puffing down the road with his Huggies.

The cop car careens onto the street in the background, its siren wailing.

The PASSENGER COP *is leaning far out his window, one hand gripping the light-and-siren rack, the other pointing a gun at* HI, *shooting away.*

Bullets whizz past.

Suddenly, with a soft pthunk! the Huggies box pops forward, out from under HI's *arm—hit by a bullet. Still running,* HI *reaches forward, tries to catch it on the fly, bobbles it, tips it—loses it. He overruns it a couple steps before he can bring himself up short.*

He turns and reaches to pick up the box but—PING-PING—bullets chew up the road near his hand.

Leaving the Huggies, HI *takes off through a well-manicured yard.*

The police car is proceeding on down the street to catch him around the corner, the driver still drawling over his loudspeaker:

SPEAKER: That's private property, son. Come back out
to the street and reveal yourself to Officer Steensma and
Officer Scott—that's me.

YARD

HI vaults a fence to land in the backyard.
*As he straightens to his feet we hear a horrible snarling
and barking.*
*A huge black Doberman is bounding across the lawn. It
looks like it means to rip HI's throat out.*

LOW TRACKING SHOT   TOWARD HI

The dog's racing POV as it bounds toward the paralyzed HI.
The dog leaps—camera flying up toward HI's face—and:

CLOSE SHOT   HI'S FROZEN PROFILE

*The dog's slavering muzzle flies into frame and—stops, bare
inches from HI's nose, and the dog falls back, having reached
the end of his chain.*
HI resumes running.

CLOSE

*On the dog, snarling and straining against the end of his
chain.*

TRACKING

*Down along the chain toward the spike mooring it to the
ground. As the dog strains, the spike starts to stir in the
ground.*
*Other dogs can be heard barking now, the Doberman
having started a sympathetic wave.*

ED'S CAR

Her jaw set, she takes a hard turn, looking this way and that.

ED: That son of a bitch . . .

The police car approaches and roars by, the PASSENGER COP *still hanging out his window.*

. . . Lookie Nathan, a police car . . .

She is looking in her rearview mirror.

. . . Say, that looks like Bill Steensma.

LOW TRACKING SHOT

The camera is shooting forward at ground level, following the Doberman as it bounds along. The Doberman is dragging his chain and spike, which stretch into the foreground, bumping and scraping along the road.

Far ahead we can see HI *running, then turning down an intersecting street.*

A second dog peels into the road to bound along with the Doberman.

TRACKING BEHIND HI

Running up a dark street. There is an oncoming pickup. HI *runs directly at it.*

INT   PICKUP

The DRIVER *screams and brakes—not quite in time.*

HI *rolls onto the hood, and off, and gamely trots over to open the passenger door.*

The DRIVER *is leaning over to tell him:*

DRIVER: Son, you got a panty on your head.

HI: Just drive fast . . .

He is displaying his gun as he starts to climb in.

. . . and don't stop till I tell ya.

Before HI *can get his door shut the* DRIVER *is obediently peeling out.*
   HI *is reacting to an oncoming car. He peels the stocking off to look, and leans across the* DRIVER's *lap to bellow as* ED's *car passes:*

HI: . . . Honey!

HI *turns to look through the back window.*

HIS POV

ED's *car is braking and spinning into a U-turn.*

BACK TO HI

Leaning out the window.

HI: Mind the baby now!

Next to him, the DRIVER *is screaming.*
   As HI *turns forward, the entire windshield explodes in.*

THEIR POV

The pimply-faced CASHIER *from the 7-Eleven is standing in the middle of the road ahead, sighting down his .44 Magnum for another shot.*
   We are rushing in.

THE DRIVER

Still screaming.

THE CASHIER

Ready to fire and—THUMP—he is bowled over by the arriving Doberman, still trailing chain and spike, and now

accompanied by three other dogs, all braying at the top of
their lungs.

   Still screaming, the DRIVER puts his body into a hard right
turn to avoid the CASHIER and hellhounds.

NEW STREET

Roaring up the new street, they are now directly in the path
of the oncoming police car, its siren wailing, barreling
straight at them.

   Still screaming, the DRIVER leans into another hard right.
Wind is whistling in through where the windshield used to
be.

   Two wheels hop curb as the car skids into the new street,
fishtails, and roars away.

ED'S CAR

She hears dogs, siren, squealing brakes on an adjacent street.

ED: Hold on Nathan, we'll take a shortcut.

She gives the wheel a hard right turn.

   But there is no cross street. The car hops the curb and roars
up someone's nicely tended front yard, heading for the gap
between this house and the one next door.

POLICE CAR

Recovered and turned around from its near collision with the
SCREAMING DRIVER, the squad car is now squealing onto the
street the SCREAMER swerved on to—resuming pursuit.

   As the police car roars down the street, ED's car appears
from between two houses behind it, bounces down the front
yard to the street and follows the police.

SCREAMER'S PICKUP

Raking two-shot of HI and the SCREAMER. HI is looking back
over his shoulder at the pursuing police.

   Desperately pleading:

SCREAMER: Can I stop now?

HI looks forward.

HIS POV

They are rushing toward an imposing colonial house planted at the end of the dead-end street.

BACK TO HI

HI: Maybe you better.

CLOSE SHOT   BRAKE PEDAL

Stepped on hard. The brakes scream.

EXT   CAR

As the car squeals to a halt HI is catapulted through where the windshield used to be, tumbling over the hood onto the front lawn.

He rolls to his feet and, as he runs up the lawn, calls back over his shoulder:

HI: Thank you.

INTO THE HOUSE

We are tracking behind HI as he runs up to the house and crashes through the screen door.

Still tracking behind him as he runs through the living room.

A middle-aged couple sits on the couch watching TV. They look up as HI rushes by.

HI plunges down a staircase. As he does so we hear: ka-chick ka-chock ka-chick ka-chock.

He emerges into a rec room where he and we rush past two kids playing ping-pong. He runs out the back door.

TRACKING WITH THE POLICEMAN

As he runs into the house.

As he runs through the living room we catch a glimpse of the middle-aged couple gaping at him.

OFFICER STEENSMA *plunges down the stairs.*

TRACKING ON HI

Outdoors now, running, crossing the street behind the house and entering the parking lot of a supermarket on the other side.

BACK TO THE HOUSE

As a pack of dogs thunders in. The lead Doberman with chain and spike has now picked up about a dozen neighborhood dogs.

The dogs thunder through the living room and down the stairs. As they hit the rec room the thunder of their feet turns into the clatter of nails on tile.

INT SUPERMARKET

As HI *bursts in. Tracking on him as he runs down the broad front aisle, head whipping as he runs, looking up each perpendicular lane, searching for something.*

He turns up one of the last lanes, races along it and grabs a carton of Huggies, still on the flat run.

He emerges into the broad back aisle and runs along it, but at the first perpendicular lane he hits, we see OFFICER STEENSMA, *gun leveled, at the other end. He fires.*

HI *keeps running.*

The POLICEMAN *is running along the front aisle, keeping pace with* HI *running along the back aisle. He squeezes off shots at* HI *as each lane gives him the opportunity.*

HI *abruptly stops between lanes and doubles back, losing the* POLICEMAN. *He runs down the second lane he comes to toward the front of the store.*

Cameraman Barry Sonnenfeld with Joel Coen and Ethan Coen

The pack of dogs appears at the end of the lane and thunders up toward HI, *braying at the top of their doggy lungs. The lead Doberman holds in his teeth a paper 7-Eleven cap.*

HI *reverses again, and emerges into the back aisle.*

BANG! A pyramid of cranberry juice explodes at his shoulder. The POLICEMAN *has been waiting at the end of the back aisle; he aims once again.*

HI *plunges down the next lane but is brought up short as KA-BOOM! five jars of applesauce explode in front of him.* HI *looks.*

Standing in the raised platform-cubicle at the front of the store is the STORE MANAGER, *a fat man in a white short-sleeved shirt with a lit cigarette dangling from his mouth.*

The MANAGER *cracks open his shotgun and inserts two more cartridges—thoonk thoonk—in the smoking chamber.*

HI *doubles back once again toward the back aisle.*

He is still several paces from the end of the lane when the POLICEMAN *appears there, squaring to face him.*

The POLICEMAN is in front of him. The MANAGER is blowing out groceries on the shelves behind him.

CLOSE ON POLICEMAN

As he coolly levels his police special and takes aim at HI.

POLICEMAN'S POV

Still on the dead run, HI is flinging the carton of Huggies. The carton rockets straight at the camera.

BACK TO POLICEMAN

Futilely raising his gun to avoid—impact: The Huggies catch him square on the chest. The force makes him stumble one fatal step backwards—into the back aisle—where:
   CRASH—He is hit broadside and bowled over by a rocketing shopping cart, propelled by an hysterically screaming SHOPPER.

TRACKING ON SHOPPER

Racing on down the back aisle, bellowing.

HER FEET

Tracking from in front. Beyond her we can see the pack of furiously barking dogs, nipping at her heels. They boil over the prostrate OFFICER STEENSMA, and this is the last we see of him in this movie.

EXT STORE

As HI emerges through the back door. ED is just skidding around the corner.
   HI scrambles in the passenger side.

INT CAR

Raking two-shot with HI in the foreground. The car peels out of the lot.

HI: Thank you honey, you really didn't have to do this—

THWAK—ED gives him a good hard slap and HI's head rolls toward the camera.

ED: You son of a bitch! You're actin' like a mad dog!

Rubbing his jaw:

HI: Turn left, honey.

Still at top speed, she leans into a hard left, tires squealing.

ED: What if me'n the baby'd been picked up? Nathan Jr. would a been accessory to armed robbery!

HI: Nawww honey, it ain't armed robbery if the gun ain't loaded—

ED: What kind of home life is this for a toddler?! You're supposed to be an example!

HI: Now honey, I never postured myself as the three-piece suit type—Turn left, dear.

ED: We got a child now, everything's changed!

HI: Well Nathan Jr. accepts me for what I am and I think you better had, too. You know, honey, I'm okay you're okay? That-there's what it is.

ED: I know, but honey—

HI: See I come from a long line of frontiersmen and—here it is, turn here dear—frontiersmen and outdoor types.

HI's eyes are fixed on something in the road ahead.

ED: I'm not gonna live this way, Hi. It just ain't family life!

HI's attention is still on the road. He is opening his door, even though the car is still racing along. He absently concedes:

HI: Well . . . It ain't Ozzie and Harriet.

LOW ANGLE   THE STREET

In the extreme foreground sits the first carton of Huggies that HI dropped in the middle of the road. The car is approaching.
    As the car passes the carton, HI's hand reaches from the passenger door and snags it.

REVERSE

As HI pulls the carton in and slams his door shut. Crane up on the car speeding away.

TRAILER LIVING ROOM

As ED bursts in the front door, holding NATHAN JR.

ED: You two are leaving.

ON GALE AND EVELLE

They look up, dumbstruck and mortified, from the sofa where they have been watching TV.

ED: Tomorrow morning. Now I got nothing against you personally . . .

GALE and EVELLE look appealingly toward HI, who shifts uncomfortably behind ED.

ED: . . . but you're wanted by the authorities and you're a bad influence in this household, in my opinion.

GALE: Well ma'am . . . we sure didn't mean to influence anyone.

EVELLE: And if we did, we apologize.

ED is unmoved.

ED: I'm goin' in to town tomorrow to see about some shots for the baby. When I come back you better be gone or I'll kick you out myself.

She storms into the bedroom and slams the door.
    There is an awkward silence as GALE studies his thumb and EVELLE stares at the ceiling. Finally EVELLE turns to HI.

EVELLE: . . . What's he need, his dip-tet?

HI: I'm awful sorry boys, but when Ed gets mad, you know, when she gets an idea . . .

GALE: Well there ain't a thing to apologize for, H.I. . .

He looks at EVELLE.

    . . . It seems pretty clear what the situation is here.

EVELLE: Yeah, I guess the Missus wants us to clear out.

GALE: Now H.I., you'll pardon me for sayin' so, but I get the feelin' that this-here . . .

His gesture seems to take in the trailer and the entire domestic situation.

. . . ain't exactly workin' out.

HI: Well now Ed's generally a real sweetheart, I—

GALE: And as per usual, I wouldn't be surprised if the source of the marital friction was financial.

HI: Well, matter of fact, I did lose my job today—

EVELLE: Come on Hi, you're young, you got your health—what do you want with a job?

GALE: But look, I'd rather light a candle than curse your darkness. As you know, Evelle'n I never go anywhere without a reason . . . and here we are in your little domicile. We come to invite you in on a score.

EVELLE: A bank, Hi.

HI is shaking his head.

HI: Aw boys, I don't—

GALE: I know you're partial to convenience stores but, H.I., the sun don't rise and set on the corner grocery.

EVELLE: It's like Doc Schwartz says: You gotta have a little ambition. Why we just heard on the news how somebody snatched off one of the Arizona babies. Now there's someone thinkin' big.

GALE: And here you are sittin' around on your butt playin' house with a—don't get me wrong, H.I., with a fine woman—but a woman who needs the button-down type.

HI: Well now that ain't really any of your—

GALE: Just lookahere . . .

He is handing HI *a folded-up picture.*

EVELLE: Picture of El Dorado, Hi.

GALE: Though the locals call it the Farmers and Mechanics Bank of LaGrange. Looks like a hayseed bank and, tell you the truth, it *is* a hayseed bank. Except the last Friday of every financial quarter there's more cash in that bank than flies at a barbecue.

EVELLE: And guess what day it is tomorrow?

GALE: Ya see, H.I., it's when the hayseeds come in to cash their farm subsidy checks.

EVELLE: A-One information.

GALE: Got it in the joint from a guy named Lawrence Spivey, one of Dick Nixon's undersecretaries of agriculture.

EVELLE: He's in for solicitin' sex from a state trooper.

GALE: Ordinarily we don't associate with that class of person, but . . .

GALE *chuckles.*

    . . . he was tryin' to make brownie points with some of the boys.

HI: Boys, I can't—

EVELLE: We need someone handy with a scatter-gun to cover the hayseeds while we get the cash.

GALE: Y'understand, H.I., if this works out it's just the beginning of a spree across the entire Southwest proper. We keep goin' till we can retire—or we get caught.

EVELLE: Either way we're fixed for life.

HI is still shaking his head.

HI: Boys, it's a kind offer, but you're suggesting I just up'n leave Ed. Now that'd be pretty damn cowardly, wouldn't it.

GALE: Would it? Think about it, H.I. Seems to me, stayin' here, y'ain't doin' her any good. And y'ain't bein' true to your own nature.

The camera has floated in to a close shot of HI, staring glumly at GALE.

TRACKING ON MOTORCYCLE   NIGHT

Following it, very close, we see only its rear wheel and fender and twin exhaust pipes, one on either side. Flame is boiling in each exhaust pipe as the hog roars.

HIGHER TRACKING SHOT

From behind the BIKER's head as he rides through the night. With the sharp whipcrack effect he suddenly looks left, searching. With a second whipcrack effect he suddenly looks right, still searching.
He banks into a turn.

EXT TRAILER

Creeping in. Late at night. We are tracking in toward the one window that is illuminated, with a feeble yellow light.
  In voice-over, HI is composing a letter.

VO: My dearest Edwinna. Tonight as you and Nathan slumber, my heart is filled with anguish . . .

DISSOLVE THROUGH TO:
INT TRAILER

Creeping in on HI's hunched back, as he sits over the kitchen table writing the letter. The yellow lamp sitting on the table is the only light on in the trailer.

VO: . . . I hope that you will both understand, and forgive me for what I have decided I must do. By the time you read this, I will be gone.

DISSOLVE THROUGH TO:
LIVING ROOM

Creeping in on GALE and EVELLE, sprawled on the sofa and easy chair respectively, sawing boards.

VO: . . . I will never be the man that you want me to be, the husband and father that you and Nathan deserve . . .

DISSOLVE THROUGH:
BACK TO HI

Still creeping in.

VO: Maybe it's my upbringing; maybe it's just that my genes got screwed up—I don't know . . .

DISSOLVE THROUGH TO:
INT 7-ELEVEN

Creeping in on the pimply-faced CASHIER, *sitting asleep behind the counter, a dirty magazine lying face-down, open on his chest.*

VO:　　But the events of the last day have showed, amply, that I don't have the strength of character to raise up a family . . .

We are slowly panning over to the newspaper rack, revealing tomorrow's headline: WHERE IS NATHAN JR.?

. . . in the manner befitting a responsible adult, and not like the wild man from Borneo.

DISSOLVE THROUGH TO:
ARIZONA HOME

Creeping in on NATHAN SR. *in the living room, asleep in his ottoman armchair, lit only by the snow from the TV set he is facing, a half-full glass of milk on the coffee table next to him.*
　　His robe is disheveled; his eyeglasses have slid down his nose.

VO:　　. . . I say all this to my shame.

DISSOLVE THROUGH TO:
TRAILER BEDROOM

Creeping in on ED *and* NATHAN JR., *asleep together in the double bed.* ED's *arm is draped protectively over the sleeping infant.*

VO:　　. . . I will love you always, truly and deeply. But I fear that if I stay I would only bring bad trouble . . .

We start to hear the rumble of the motorcycle mix up again.

. . . on the heads of you and Nathan Jr.

DISSOLVE THROUGH TO:
BLACKNESS

Night sky. The motorcycle tire enters frame as the bike comes to a halt. The BIKER *plants a jackbooted foot in the foreground.*
    The engine rumbles.

VO: I feel the thunder gathering even now; if I leave, hopefully, it will leave with me.

We are craning up over the BIKER's *back to reveal what he is looking at: We are on a bluff overlooking the trailer park. In the window of one trailer below, a yellow light glows.*

. . . I cannot tarry . . .

DISSOLVE THROUGH:
BACK TO HI

Still creeping in.

VO: Better I should go, send you money, and let you curse my name. Your loving . . . Herbert.

FADE OUT
FIRE

Roaring at the cut. Through it we can see the BIKER *sitting on the ground, legs stretched out in front of him, back resting against his parked motorcycle, arms folded across his chest.*
    Perfectly motionless, he stares at the campfire.
    We are floating in toward him.
    As we come closer, eventually drawing in to a close shot of his face, we gradually realize something peculiar about his

eyes: *He seems to have none. Although his eyes are unblinkingly open we do not see eyeballs, but only fire— either a reflection of the campfire or something roaring— burning—inside.*

CLOSE SHOT   DOOR MAT

It reads: "Come On In! To Unpainted Arizona."
   The smoking butt of a cheroot is dropped onto the mat. A jackbooted foot grinds it out.

CLOSE SHOT   BAR ON GLASS DOOR

Leading into the showroom. The BIKER's *mail-and-chained fist pushes the door open.*

LOW WIDE TRACKING SHOT

Behind the jackboots as they stroll through a showroom of unpainted furniture and bathroom fixtures.

TRACKING ON THE MAILED HAND

Swinging as he walks, the BIKER's *hand produces a fresh cheroot from no apparent source—either sleight-of-hand or magic.*

THE OTHER HAND

Similarly producing a long wooden match.

DISCOLORED TEETH

Biting down on the cigar.

HAND

Dragging the kitchen match along the unfinished wood surface of an expensive bureau, leaving an ugly black scar. The match erupts into roaring flame.

CIGAR

Crackling as it is lit.

DOOR

Reading "Executive Offices." The mailed fist pushes it open.

PEBBLED GLASS DOOR

From the inside of the office. The name on the pebbled glass is a backwards NATHAN ARIZONA.

There is the shadow of a man approaching the door, and muffled voices.

SECRETARY'S VOICE: I'm sorry, Mr. Arizona, he just barged in . . .

The door swings open and NATHAN *stands looking in, his middle-aged secretary hanging at his elbow.*

. . . Should I call Dewayne?

NATHAN *is staring toward his desk.*

NATHAN: Hell no, why wake the security guard. I'll take care a this.

The secretary leaves.

NATHAN'S POV

The BIKER *sits with his back to us, jackboots propped lazily on the desk.*

His head bobs and ducks, as if he is following some movement in the air in front of him.

BACK TO NATHAN

Eyes on the BIKER *he slams the door shut behind him, looking for some reaction.*

BIKER

No reaction. His head continues to bob and duck.

BACK TO NATHAN

Circling the BIKER as he crosses to sit behind his desk.

HIS POV

Arcing around to reveal the BIKER's face. He still does not react to NATHAN, not even bothering to give him a glance. His eyes continue to follow some phantom movement.

When the BIKER speaks it is still without looking at NATHAN, and with a surprisingly soft voice and mild, unhurried manner:

BIKER: You got flies.

He finally looks at NATHAN, and smiles faintly.

NATHAN: I doubt it. This place's climate-controlled, all the windows are sealed. Who the hell are you?

BIKER: Name of Leonard Smalls. My friends call me Lenny . . .

He takes a drag on his cigar.

. . . Only I ain't got no friends.

NATHAN: Stop, you'll make me bust out crying. Listen Leonard, you want some furniture or a shitbox, they're out on the sales floor.

SMALLS is pleasantly shaking his head.

SMALLS: Nooo, I ain't a customer, I'm a manhunter. Ordinarily. Though I do hunt babies, on occasion. Hear you got one you can't put your hand to.

NATHAN: What do you know about it?

SMALLS: Wal, that's my business. I'm a tracker—part Hopi Indian, some say part hound dog. When some dink skips bail, crushes outta the joint, I'm the man they call.

NATHAN: Mister, I got the cops, the state troopers and the Federal-B-I already lookin' for my boy. Now if you got information I *strongly* advise—

SMALLS: Cop won't find your boy. Cop couldn't find his own butt if it had a bell on it. Wanna find an outlaw, call an outlaw. Wanna find a Dunkin Donuts, call a cop.

NATHAN: Smalls, first off, take your damn feet off m'furniture. Second off, it's widely known I posted a twenty grand reward for my boy. If you can find him, claim it. Short of that what do we got to talk about?

SMALLS: Price. Fair price. And that ain't whatever you say it is; fair price is what the market'll bear. Now there are people, mind you, there are people in this land, who'll pay a lot more'n twenty grand for a healthy baby.

NATHAN is looking at him stonily.

NATHAN: What're you after?

SMALLS: Give you an idea, when I was a lad I m'self fetched twenty-*five* thousand on the black market. And them's 1954 dollars. I'm sayin, fair price. For *fifty* grand I'll track him, find him—

Quick as a flash the heretofore languid SMALLS bolts forward, his fist stopped an inch short of NATHAN's nose.

EXTREME CLOSE SHOT   SMALLS' FINGERS

His index finger and thumb are pinched together—holding the leg of a struggling fly that he has just plucked from the air.

SMALLS: . . . and the people that took him . . .

He flicks the fly away.

. . . I'll kick their butts.

He sits back down.

. . . No extra charge.

NATHAN stares grimly at SMALLS.

NATHAN: And if I don't pay?

SMALLS: Oh I'll get your boy regardless. Cause if *you* don't pay, the market will.

NATHAN: You wanna know what I think? I think you're an evil man. I think this is nothin' but a goddamn screw job. I think it's a shakedown. I think you're the one took Nathan Jr. and my fine friend, I think you're the one gonna get his butt kicked . . .

NATHAN swivels to punch numbers on a telephone.

. . . I think I'm on the phone to the cops right now, and I—

He swivels back, looking up, and his speech stops short.

HIS POV

The office is empty. A whipcrack effect builds to the cut and:

CLOSE ON HI

His eyes snap open as the whipcrack echoes away.
He has been slumped over the kitchen table, asleep.

GALE (*os*):   Up and attem, H.I. Today is the first day of the rest of your life . . .

EVELLE (*os*):   . . . and already you're fuckin' it up.

HI looks up.
GALE and EVELLE are smiling down at him.

EVELLE: Come on, the missus'll be back from town soon.

HI takes the envelope that he was slumped over, TO ED written on its face. As he sticks it to the refrigerator door with a broccoli magnet:

HI: Where's the baby?

EVELLE: Bedroom, in his crib.

GALE: He's sawin' toothpicks, he'll be fine.

There is a harsh knock at the door. All three tense.

. . . You expectin' anybody?

HI is staring. The knock comes again.

HI: No. You two stay outta sight.

He goes to the door, pulls back its shade and peeks out. Under his breath:

HI: Shit.

He opens the door.

EXT TRAILER

It is GLEN. *He backs nervously down to the foot of the stoop as* HI *stands in the half-open doorway.* GLEN *comes to rest a few feet away from the stoop.*
    He is wearing a neckbrace. The bridge of his eyeglasses is taped together. Cotton wadding is stuffed up his nose, which is darkly discolored. He holds a rolled up newspaper.
    His station wagon is parked behind him, idling.

HI: Morning Glen.

GLEN *speaks in a very nasal voice:*

GLEN: I ain't comin' in if ya don't mind. I'll just keep my distance.

HI: I didn't invite you in, Glen.

GLEN: Well don't even bother. First off, you're fired— and that's official.

HI: I kinda figured that, Glen.

GLEN: Well that ain't why I'm here neither. No sir. You're in a whole shitload of trouble, my friend.

    HI is looking at him evenly.

HI: Why don't you just calm down, Glen.

GLEN: Why don't you make me?! Know that little baby you got in there? Remember him? I know what his real name is!

HI is suddenly nervous and urgent:

HI: Wanna keep your voice down, Glen?

GLEN: I'll pitch my voice wherever I please! His name ain't Hi Jr.! His name ain't Ed Jr.! But it's Junior all right! Yes sir, it's *Nathan* Jr.!

HI takes one step down holding out a calming hand.
GLEN takes two nervous steps away and reassures himself by resting a hand on the door of his station wagon.

. . . Stay away from me, McDunnough!

HI stops short. GLEN smiles.

GLEN: . . . Sure, you're an awful big man when you got somethin' around to clobber a guy with!

HI (*softly*):   I ain't a big man.

GLEN: That's right! And now you're at my mercy!

He spits on the dirt in front of him.

. . . I'm your worst nightmare! I wanted to just turn you in for the re-ward. But Dot, she wants something to cuddle. So it looks like that baby's gonna be *Glen* Jr. from now on!

HI's face is set in rigid dismay.

. . . I'll give you a day to break the news to Ed . . .

GLEN *is getting into his car.*

. . . Dot'll be by tomorrow to pick him up.

He slams the door.

. . . It's either that or jail. Oh and say, that reminds me! You'll find a doctor bill in the mail in a few days. I recommend you pay it!

And the car squeals off.
    HI *looks back at the trailer.*

HIS POV

A slat in the window blind drops back into place.

BACK TO HI

He opens the door.

INT   TRAILER

EVELLE *is already emerging from the bedroom with the baby in his arms.*
    HI *moves toward* EVELLE. *His teeth are set; he means business.*

HI: What's goin' on here.

GALE *steps in front of* HI.

GALE: You know what's goin' on, H.I. It's just business. Now this can go either hard or easy—

HI gives GALE *a hard push to get past him.* GALE *staggers back but recovers and grabs* HI *in a bear hug.*
    HI *flips* GALE. GALE *lands on a coffee table which flips up and crashes back down.*

EVELLE *is dancing back out of* HI's *reach. As* HI *lunges for him the prostrate* GALE *grabs his legs.*

HI *goes down hard.*

GALE *leaps to his feet and—CRASH—bangs his head up against an overhanging lamp. Both of his hands fly up to massage the top of his head.*

THOOMP—HI's *fist flies into frame to connect with* GALE's *unguarded stomach.* GALE *doubles over, clutching at his gut.*

HI *interlaces his fingers to make a club of his two hands. With* GALE's *bowed head a target in front of him,* HI *swings his hands up over his head.*

HI's *knuckles scrape painfully against the plaster of the too-low ceiling. Skin is flayed, plaster crumbles.*

HI *grabs at his knuckles in pain.* GALE *lunges with a mid-body tackle that sends* HI *crashing into the wall.*

GALE, *still on top of him, reaches back to throw a punch. The reach-back sends his elbow crashing through a window but doesn't stop the punch.*

It connects with HI's *jaw.*

GALE *throws another quick punch, all his weight behind it.* HI's *head bobs sideways just in time and* GALE's *fist goes through the wall. It is momentarily stuck there.*

HI *uses the opportunity to grab* GALE's *one free arm with both of his. He is twisting it to make* GALE, *roaring with pain, twist around and present his back to him.*

HI *climbs aboard, grabbing* GALE's *face.*

GALE, *still roaring, is pulling his fist out of the hole. He grabs a lath exposed by the hole and pulls; it tears out of the wall and snaps free, giving him a length of about two feet.*

GALE *is rampaging around like a grizzly bear hemmed in a too-small space.* HI *is hanging on for dear life, his own feet flailing this way and that, knocking over lamps and wall fixtures as* GALE *bends and twirls about, trying to shake him loose.* GALE *crashes and bounces off the walls, roaring in pain and fury.*

Close shots of GALE's *face show his features impossibly and grotesquely contorted by* HI's *hand, squeezing, gripping and clutching at it.*

EVELLE *is dancing around with the baby, dodging crashing furniture and flailing body parts.*

EXT   WIDE SHOT   THE TRAILER

At the cut GALE's *roaring drops out. We hear the chirping of birds and the laughter of children playing in the neighborhood.*

It is a sunny day.

BACK TO INT TRAILER

GALE *still roars. With a last mighty effort, he finally swings* HI *off his body.*

HI *crashes against a wall and through it to land in the:*

BATHROOM

Amid a shower of plaster dust and lath. HI *has landed, groggily, against the toilet.*

EVELLE *enters now with his hands free, apparently having set the baby down somewhere.*

He yanks the cord off the bathroom blinds.

LIVING ROOM

HI *is seated in a straight-back chair, still violently struggling but* GALE's *arms are wrapped around him from behind.*

EVELLE *is just finishing tying off his wrists behind the chair.*

No one talks; there is nothing left to say.

Finished, GALE *goes to the door and* EVELLE *goes to the bedroom. He emerges with the baby and precedes* GALE *out the door,* GALE *slamming it behind him.*

HI *starts bucking and struggling, weeping tears of rage and frustration. He succeeds only in tipping forward, face down into the carpet, the strapped-on chair pressing down on top of him.*

His profile is pressed into the carpet.

Offscreen we hear the door of the trailer opening.

HI'S POV

At carpet level. GALE's *shoes enter his field of vision. They stride over to a mess of debris in the corner of the living room.*

OBJECTIVE SHOT

As GALE *paws through the wreckage to expose the copy of Dr. Spock's* Baby and Child Care. *He grabs the book.*

HI'S POV

The feet walk away and leave his field of vision.

CLOSE ON HI

As we hear the door slam shut with horrible finality.

HI's *mouth stretches wide. He ROARS with grief and frustration.*

WIDE SHOT

Moving down the road toward an oncoming car. As the oncoming car gets closer we can see GALE *and* EVELLE *in its front seat.*

As the car passes we pan with it, to reveal that we have been shooting from the inside of another car, and we hold on the profile of its driver: ED. *She has just watched the other car shoot past.*

ED: . . . Good.

QUICK FADE OUT

INT   DEVASTATED TRAILER

As ED *sits heavily into frame, apparently in shock, her frozen profile to the camera as she stares straight ahead into space.*

Her foreground hand absently holds a length of cord.
    Beyond her in the middle background HI *is rummaging in the debris. He stands up, cropped from the chest down and starts loading bullets into the chamber of* ED's *.38 police special.*

HI (*frantically*):   I know you're worried honey but believe me, there ain't a thing to worry about. We're absolutely gonna get him back, there just ain't no question about that . . .

He snaps the chamber shut and leaves frame, still talking.

    . . . We'll get him back, that's just all there is to it. And you wanna know another thing?

He is walking back into frame holding another handgun now in addition to the .38, this one an automatic.

    . . . I'm gonna be a better person from here on out. And that's final, I mean that's absolutely the way it's gonna be, that's official. You were right and I was wrong . . .

He snaps a clip into the automatic.

HI: . . . A blind man could tell you that. Now they ain't gonna hurt him, they're just in it for the score . . .

HI *is leaving frame again, continuing to talk as we hear him rummaging offscreen.*

    . . . But I ain't like that no more, I'm a changed man. You were right and I was wrong. We got a family here and I'm gonna start acting responsibly . . .

HI *enters frame with the two handguns stuck in his belt, holding his pump-action shotgun.*

. . . So let's go honey . . .

He primes the shotgun: WHOOSH-CLACK.

. . . Let's go get Nathan Jr.

TRACKING SHOT

From the front bumper of an automobile. Beautiful desert stretches to the horizon. The road rushes under the camera.

GALE AND EVELLE'S CAR

GALE drives, gazing out at the road. EVELLE holds NATHAN JR., occasionally bouncing him. Contemplatively:

GALE: I luuuuv to drive.

EVELLE: You said somethin' there, pardner.

GALE: . . . Yessir, I figure with the ransom and this bank, you'n I'll be sittin' in the fabled catbird seat.

EVELLE is looking down at the baby, shifting him in his lap.

EVELLE: Uh, Gale . . . Junior had a, uh, accident.

GALE: What's that, pardner?

EVELLE: He had a little accident.

GALE looks over.

GALE: Wuddya mean, he looks okay.

EVELLE: No, ya see . . . Movin' though we are, he just had hisself a rest stop.

GALE: Well it's perfectly natural.

EVELLE (*very excited*):   Hey Gale!

GALE: What now?

EVELLE, *beaming, looks up from the baby to* GALE.

EVELLE: . . . He smiled at me!

THE SUN

A huge rumbling rippling red ball that fills the frame.
As we hear his footfalls on concrete steps, SMALLS *rises into frame, apparently climbing a stoop. The sun behind him throws him into silhouette; the extreme telephoto flattens him against the sun. Heat waves ripple between us and him, making his figure slightly waver.*
The rumble builds, louder and louder, until it is snapped off by a—

INT TRAILER

—CLICK. The front door handle clicks open and SMALLS *stands in the doorway. The abandoned trailer is perfectly quiet.*
The room is a complete shambles from the fight. Sunlight filters in between the slats of the venetian blinds. Smoke from LENNY SMALLS' *cheroot ripples up through the light.*
After only a momentary pause at the door to take in the scene, SMALLS *goes directly to a specific spot in the debris and nudges some of it aside with his toe, exposing a piece of paper.*
He bends down to pick it up but suddenly freezes, with a soft grunt of surprise.

HIS POV

At knee-height on the wall in front of him, "FART" is scrawled in crayon.

BACK TO SMALLS

As he stands up with the piece of paper.

THE PAPER

It is GALE's picture of the Farmers and Mechanics Bank.

INT CONVENIENCE STORE

Close on a carton of diapers being set down on the check-out counter.

EVELLE (os):   Know how you put these thangs on?

WIDER

EVELLE and the CASHIER, a late-middle-aged man (perhaps the proprietor of this small mom-and-pop store) face each other across the check-out counter. EVELLE has various baby purchases—the diapers, baby food, etc.—piled on the counter. The CASHIER is ringing them up.

  Through the open door beyond them we can see a strip of the parking lot.

CASHIER: Welp. Around the butt, then up over the groin area—

EVELLE: I know *where* they go, old timer. I mean do I need pins or fasteners?

We see GALE trotting past through the visible part of the parking lot, cooing "Weeeeee!" as he holds NATHAN JR. up over his head.

CASHIER: Well no, they got those tape-ettes already on there, it's self-contained and fairly explanatory.

EVELLE: Uh-huh . . .

He takes a plastic-covered squirt gun off a display rack and drops it on the counter. He is looking around at the other impulse purchases displayed by the register; he unhooks a bag of balloons.

. . . These blow up into funny shapes at all?

GALE is trotting by in the opposite direction: "Weeeeee!"

CASHIER:　Well no. Unless round is funny.

EVELLE is pulling a gun out of his belt.

EVELLE:　All right, I'll take these too. Now you lie down back there—

CASHIER:　Yessir!

EVELLE:　—and don't you move till you've counted up to eight hundred and twenty-five and then backwards down to zero. I'll be back to check—see y'ain't cheatin'.

The CASHIER is already down on the floor, out of frame.

CASHIER (os):　You the diaper burglar?

As he heads for the door with the groceries:

EVELLE:　Looks like I'm one of 'em.

EXT STORE

As EVELLE hurriedly emerges with the two bags. Faintly we can hear the CASHIER bellowing: "One one thousand, two one thousand . . ."

EVELLE:　Get the door, will ya?

GALE is slipping the baby back into his car seat, which sits on the roof of the car. He starts doing up the straps.

GALE: He's a real cheerful little critter once he warms up to ya.

Hands free now, GALE reaches for the back door.

EVELLE: Hurry up Gale . . .

GALE has the door open. EVELLE starts throwing in the groceries.

. . . I don't know how high this one can count.

GALE AND EVELLE'S CAR

GALE drives as EVELLE sorts through his purchases.

EVELLE: Got him some baby grub . . . baby wipes . . . diapers, disposable . . . packet of balloons—

GALE: They blow up into funny shapes at all?

EVELLE: No, just—

GALE is looking around, puzzled.

GALE: Say, where's Junior?

EVELLE: Wuddya mean, didn't you put him in?!

GALE: No, I thought—

The two men look at each other.

REVERSE

The two men's heads whip around to look in the back seat.

BACK TO FRONT ANGLE

They look at each other in horror.

GALE: Where'd we leave him?!

The two men's eyes widen as they remember at the same time: both look up at the roof of the car.

CLOSE ON GALE'S FOOT

Coming off the accelerator.

CLOSE ON EVELLE

Screaming as he watches the foot:

EVELLE: NOOOOOO!!

—But too late.

GALE'S FOOT

Already plunging down on the brake. SQUEEEEEEEAL . . .

TWO SHOT

EVELLE is screaming at the top of his lungs as the car rocks to a stop. He peers through the windshield, still screaming, but nothing has shot off the roof of the car.

He cranes his neck to look up the slant of the windshield toward the roof. This of course gives him no view; still screaming, he thrusts his body out his open window to look up at the roof. His scream is muted as his head disappears from view, then comes back full force as he ducks back in, frantically shaking his head.

With this GALE's last hope disappears and he starts bellowing also.

GALE'S FOOT

Rising from the brake to plunge down on the accelerator.

EXT   THE CAR

As it hangs a squealing U-turn and races off at top speed.

LOW WIDE SHOT

In the foreground NATHAN JR. *sits upright in his car seat, in the middle of the road that fronts the convenience store. He is placidly looking at the scenery.*
   Faintly, we hear the CASHIER *bellowing:*

CASHIER: . . . Seven hunnert ninety-seven one thousand, seven hunnert ninety-six one thousand . . .

GALE AND EVELLE

In their speeding car, both staring out at the road ahead, mouths gaping, emitting ear-splitting screams.

INT   STORE

Shot faces the front of the store with some of the street visible outside. The CASHIER *on the floor is out of frame, but we can hear him loud and clear:*

CASHIER: . . . Seven hunnert ninety-one one thousand, seven hunnert—ah . . . bullshit.

He rises into frame, back to the camera, just as:
   We see GALE *and* EVELLE'S *car, through the front window, roaring up the street. Quick as a shot, the* CASHIER *has dropped back out of frame and resumes bellowing:*

. . . Seven hunnert ninety-ought one thousand! Seven hundred eighty—

The car is starting to squeal to a screaming halt.

BACK TO LOW WIDE SHOT

With NATHAN JR. *in the foreground.* GALE *and* EVELLE'S *car comes to a rocking halt behind—and inches shy of—the baby.*

EVELLE's *door is already open. He bolts from it and runs over to the baby, blubbering. He picks up the car seat and* NATHAN JR.
GALE *is also getting out of the car.*

EVELLE: Promise we ain't never gonna give him up, Gale! We ain't never gonna let him go!

GALE, *choked up, speaks in a low unsteady voice:*

GALE: We'll never give him up, Evelle. He's our little Gale Jr. now.

HI AND ED'S CAR

HI *driving. Both are staring wordlessly ahead at the road.*
HI *looks over at* ED, *glum but trying to be kind.*

HI: . . . Ed, I realize I can't be much of a comfort to you. But lemme just say this . . .

He is nodding to himself.

. . . You'll feel a whole lot better when—

ED: I don't wanna feel better.

HI: Honey—

ED: I don't care about myself anymore. I don't care about us anymore. I just want Nathan Junior back safe.

HI: I know that—

ED: If we don't get him back safe, I don't wanna go on livin'. And even if we do, I don't wanna go on livin' with you.

This shuts HI *up.*
   After a moment:

ED: . . . I guess I still love you Hi; I know I do. I ain't even blaming you. The whole thing was crazy and the whole thing was my idea.

   HI *clears his throat.*

HI: Well, factually, I myself bear a very large—

ED: Lemme finish. Since those jailbirds took little Nathan I been doin' some thinking, and I ain't too proud of myself. Even if Mrs. Arizona had more'n she could handle, I was a police officer sworn to uphold the Constitution of the United States—

HI: Now waitaminute honey, you resigned before we—

ED: That ain't the point, Hi. We don't deserve Nathan Jr. Any more'n those jailbirds do. And if I'm as selfish and irresponsible as you—

HI: Y'ain't *that* bad, honey.

ED: —If I'm as bad as you, what good're we to each other. You'n me's just a fool's paradise.

FARMERS AND MECHANICS BANK

Baking in the noonday sun.

GALE AND EVELLE

Sitting in the front seat of their idling car, looking at the bank.

EVELLE: There she is.

GALE: Yep. Welp . . .

They look at each other. GALE reaches for his door.

. . . Let's do her.

EVELLE: Waitaminute. What do we do with Gale Jr.?

GALE: Wuddya mean, he waits here.

EVELLE: Are you crazy?! He can't wait here by hisself. Supposin' we get killed in there—it could be hours before he's discovered.

INT   FARMERS AND MECHANICS BANK

As GALE and EVELLE bang in through the door. EVELLE holds a shotgun; GALE holds a shotgun in one hand and NATHAN JR. in his car seat in the other.

GALE: All right you hayseeds, it's a stick-up! Everbody freeze! Everbody down on the ground!

Everyone freezes, staring at GALE and EVELLE. An OLD HAYSEED with his hands in the air speaks up:

HAYSEED: Well which is it young fella? You want I should freeze or get down on the ground? Mean to say, iffen I freeze, I can't rightly drop. And iffen I drop, I'm a gonna be in motion. Ya see—

GALE: SHUTUP!

Promptly:

HAYSEED: Yessir.

GALE: Everone down on the ground!

EVELLE: Y'all can just forget that part about freezin'.

GALE: That is until they get down there.

EVELLE: Y'all hear that?

There is a murmur of acknowledgment from all the people on the ground.
GALE is tossing EVELLE a sack.

GALE: Wanna fill that sack, pardner? We got—shit!

He is looking in shock at the tellers' counter.

. . . Where'd all the tellers go?

There is no one behind the counter.
A muffled voice from offscreen:

VOICE: We're down here, sir.

EVELLE: They're down on the ground like you commanded, Gale.

GALE: I told you not to use m'damn name! Can't you even try to keep from forgettin' that?!

EVELLE is momentarily abashed, but then brightens:

EVELLE: Not even yer *code* name?

GALE registers understanding.

GALE: Oh yeah . . . m'*code* name.

EVELLE: Y'all hear that?

There is a murmur of acknowledgment from all the people on the ground.

GALE: All right now everone, we're just about ready to begin the robbery proper . . .

EXT   POLICE CAR

The camera is locked down on the roof of the rocketing squad car, looking past its flashing gumballs.
The car is approaching the townlet, its siren wailing.

BACK TO THE BANK

A teller is finishing stuffing the last of two burlap bags. Close on her hands, we see her putting in a cash packet that is really only a few bills and a sleeve surrounding and hiding a small plastic device.
The teller hits a button on the device and it starts ticking; she shoves it into the sack.

EVELLE: All right now everone, you know how this works: Y'all stay flattened for ten full minutes . . .

He is grabbing the two sacks and tosses one to GALE, who also picks up the baby. As the two are backing toward the door:

. . . We might come back in five to check. That's for us to know and y'all to find out.

GALE: Anyone found bipedal in five wears his ass for a hat.

They bolt out the door.

EXT   POLICE CAR

Siren jumps in loud at the cut. It is the same locked-down shot over the gumballs.

EXT   GALE AND EVELLE'S CAR

Peeling out from in front of the bank.

INT   GALE AND EVELLE'S CAR

GALE is driving; EVELLE starts pawing through one of the sacks.

GALE: That old timer threw off my concentration. Otherwise it would a gone smoother.

EVELLE: We done okay. Yessir. This ought to split nicely three ways.

A thought registers with GALE and EVELLE at the same moment.
They look at each other. They both twist frantically to look in the back seat.
Bellowing:

GALE: Goddamnit! Ya never leave a man behind!

KA-POP! With a loud flat crack something detonates in the front seat and the interior of the car is spattered with bright blue paint.
GALE and EVELLE, both covered in blue, are screaming in rage, fear and incomprehension. Blue dollar bills snap and flutter around the inside of the car.
The car is swerving wildly as GALE drives blind, the inside of the windshield covered with blue paint. He reaches forward to wipe clear a patch of windshield.

HIS POV

As the blue paint is smeared away we see HI and ED's car parked broadside in the middle of the road. HI and ED are in front of it, HI aiming his scatter gun, ED her revolver.
The guns spit orange flame.

HI'S POV

*Down the barrel of his shotgun. The car with the blue interior
is swerving crazily at us, one front tire blown out.*
   HI *lets go with the other barrel.*
   *The shot chews up the front grill, shatters one headlight
and blows out the other front tire. The hood of the car flies
open.*
   The car is squealing to a halt and GALE *and* EVELLE *pile
out, still bellowing.*

GALE: Goddamnit H.I., ain't we got enough to contend
with?

ED is running over to GALE *and* EVELLE's *car, throwing open
the back door to look for the baby but coming out only with
Dr. Spock's* Baby and Child Care.
   EVELLE *is staggering around in shock, looking in disbelief
at his own blue body.*

ED: Where's the baby?

EVELLE *points this way and that, in a state of confusion.*

EVELLE: I think we left him on the roof of the . . . he
must be back at the . . .

HI *and* ED *are climbing into their car.*

GALE: Let us come with! . . .

HI *and* ED *are already peeling out.*

   . . . He's our baby too!

CLOSE ON NATHAN JR.

*Sitting placidly in his car seat that sits in the middle of the
road in front of the bank.*

*We can hear the wail of the police siren still approaching.
As we hold on* NATHAN JR. *we hear the distant booming of a
shotgun.*

*As we boom up to show the empty street beyond the baby,
we hear the crack of return fire and furiously squealing
brakes. The screech culminates in a loud explosion that snaps
off the siren wail. The police car is apparently history.*

*From beyond the crest of the road ahead a ball of flame has
leapt up with the explosion. As the explosion echoes and fades
we hear the deep rumble of an approaching engine.*

LENNY SMALLS' *motorcycle appears over the rise. Framed
against fire and smoke, he is coming directly toward us, and
the baby.*

FROM BEHIND HI AND ED

*As they top a rise coming from the other direction. We see the
baby sitting in the middle of the street, and* LENNY *fast
approaching from the background.*

LOCKED DOWN TO MOTORCYCLE

*The extremely low wide shot, locked down to the speeding
bike, shows us rushing toward the rear of* NATHAN JR.'s *car
seat.*

With a clank of chains LENNY's *hand drops down into
frame, palm forward, tensing to scoop up the car seat that we
are almost upon.*

A tattoo on LENNY's *wrist reads "No Prisoners."*

REVERSE

Low shot with NATHAN JR. *in the foreground.*
He is scooped up and out of frame as LENNY *roars by.*

ON LENNY

Roaring along. He hooks the car seat over his handlebars.

Randall "Tex" Cobb (Leonard Smalls) on motorcycle

OVER HI AND ED'S SHOULDERS

LENNY is approaching. Under her breath:

ED: What is he?

HI: . . . D'you see him too?

LENNY is sawing a shotgun out of his back holster and leveling it at the oncoming car.

LENNY is sighting down the gun, swinging it around as he approaches the car.

HI and ED duck just as:

The shotgun spits orange flame and the windshield explodes in.

LENNY roars by.

LENNY'S POV

The baby on the handlebars in the foreground; the road rushing by beyond him.
   The bike banks into a hard turn.

FACING HI AND ED

Shooting through where the windshield used to be, cutting in at the end of the skid as the car rocks to a halt.
   HI *and* ED *are raising their heads. Facing forward, they do not see* LENNY *approaching again through the rear window. He is sawing out his second shotgun.*
   HI *looks around, reaches and pulls* ED *down beneath him just as:*
   Ka-BOOM!—The second shotgun roars and the back window spits in.
   As LENNY *roars past the back window he casually flips something in.*

LOOKING DOWN AT HI AND ED

*Folded over in the front seat. Below them something bounces into and around the leg well—*LENNY's *grenade.*

EXT   CAR

As the two front doors fly open and HI *and* ED *spill out—*HI *from the driver's side, heading for the far side of the road, and* ED *from the passenger side.*

ON ED

As she dives for cover behind a parked car. Beyond her— KABOOM!—their car explodes and bounces, pouring black smoke.

ON HI

The explosion flings him to the ground in the middle of the street.

THROUGH FIRE AND SMOKE

Looking up the street to where LENNY *is wheeling his bike in a U-turn. He is not finished yet.*

HI

Flat on his back, woozily shaking his head.
    He weakly raises himself on his elbows to look down the street.

HIS POV

Looking down the length of his own body. His legs stretch away in a V.
    Crashing down from a wheelie, LENNY*'s roaring bike is almost upon him—aiming up the middle of the V.*

HI

He rolls. As the bike is roaring by:

HI'S HAND

Reaches and snags a chain on LENNY*'s passing boot.*

HI

Dragged several yards before the boot shakes him off, leaving him on his stomach in the middle of the road.
    HI *looks up the road.*

HIS POV

LENNY *is again sluing the bike around.*

REAR WHEEL OF BIKE

Smoking as it skids around in the foreground, completing its turn.
    Boom up LENNY*'s back to reveal* ED *stomping straight up the street toward him—unarmed, unafraid.*

ED: I want that baby!

BACK TO HI

He reaches back to pull up his shirt, revealing a gun tucked in his pants in the small of his back. He grabs the gun.

OVER LENNY'S SHOULDER

As ED *closes in.*

ED: Gimme that baby, you warthog from hell!

LENNY's *arms rise into frame. With a roll of his wrists two knives appear in his hands.*

BACK TO HI

On his stomach, sighting down the gun toward LENNY.

HIS POV

ED *stepping into his line of fire, blocking* LENNY.

FROM BEHIND LENNY

Raising an arm to stab.
    ED *stoops to scoop the baby from the car seat, revealing:*
    HI, *behind her. He fires.*

LENNY'S HAND

Drilled by HI's *bullet, drops its knife.*
    The exit wound spurts, not flesh and blood, but a brief jet of fire.

LENNY

Quick as a flash hurling the other knife at HI.

HI

As the knife stings the gun out of his hand.

KNIFE ON THE GROUND AT LENNY'S FEET

LENNY *bends to scoop up the knife he dropped.*

TRACKING BEHIND ED

As she runs toward the bank, clutching NATHAN JR. *to her chest.*

INT   BANK

As ED *bursts in. The floor is littered with obedient hayseeds. From where he lies prone:*

OLD TIMER: Just lie down on the floor, missie.

BANG: The front door bursts open before LENNY'S *roaring hog.*
     It sails off a step into the sunken atrium, and lands with a CRASH amidst the hayseeds.

TRACKING BEHIND ED

As she runs for the back door and pushes through it.

TRACKING BEHIND LENNY

As he slaloms through the wildly scattering hayseeds.

EXT   BACK OF BANK

As LENNY *bursts out.*
     With a whipcrack effect he looks left, then right.
     He jerks the bike right, to where an alleyway flanks the side of the bank.

ALLEYWAY

ED *is running up the alley toward the front of the bank as* LENNY *enters. He roars after her.*

LENNY'S POV

Roaring down the alley.

TRACKING IN FRONT OF ED

As the bike approaches behind her.

BACK TO LENNY'S POV

Closing on ED *as she reaches the mouth of the alley.*
A plank swings into frame, straight at the camera.

REVERSE

Matching action as HI finishes swinging the plank into
LENNY's face.
    LENNY *hits the ground hard as his bike spins out from*
under him.

THE BIKE

Riderless, twisting crazily into the street where it collapses.

HI AND ED

LENNY *is rising to his feet beyond them as* HI *nods*
encouragement to ED.

HI: Run along now, honey.

    LENNY *is reaching back to throw his knife.*
    HI, *unaware, is turning to face him, presenting the plank*
as—the knife is thrown.
    It thunks into the plank, piercing it through.
    HI *backs up, swinging the knife-studded plank to make*
LENNY *keep his distance.*

TRACKING BEHIND LENNY'S SHOULDER

As he reaches up to unhook a chain from a ring on his vest
shoulder.

LENNY'S HAND

As the free chain drops down into his palm.

LENNY

Swinging the chain—whoosh whoosh—at the backpedaling HI.

THE PLANK

As the chain snakes around it and rips it out of HI*'s hands.*

LENNY

Grabbing HI *by the shirtfront.*

LENNY'S OTHER HAND

Swings down and brass knuckles appear on it.

"Tex" Cobb, Nicolas Cage, and Joel Coen

ON HI

As LENNY's *fist swings into frame to club him forehand, then backhand.*
    An uppercut from his heels sends HI *sprawling back.*

A PARKED CAR

As HI *lands against it, banging his head. He sinks to the ground.*
    LENNY *is casually walking toward him, lighting a cheroot.*
    HI *flops over onto his stomach and starts wriggling under the car.*

FROM UNDER THE CAR

HI's *face in the foreground as he desperately seeks escape.*
    Behind him we can see LENNY *casually reaching down and grabbing an ankle.*
    The shot is framed identically to the shot in the Arizona nursery where HI *pulled a baby from under the crib.*
    LENNY *pulls.* HI *is dragged away from the camera and out from under the car.*

HI

Struggling to stand up.
    LENNY *wraps his arms around him and applies a tremendous bear hug.*

HI'S ARMS

Crushed against LENNY. *His hands paw futilely at* LENNY's *chest.*

FULL SHOT

LENNY *finally flings* HI *away.*

HI

Landing in the dust, all the fight beaten out of him.

LENNY

Tired of the fight: He saws out both shotguns.

THE HAMMERS

On the guns as LENNY's *thumbs draw them back. He raises the guns to fire.*

HI

The end of the road.
  He wearily lifts a hand, defensively extending it in front of him—then stops, staring at:

HIS HAND

A hand grenade pin hangs, glinting, from one of his fingers. Pawing at LENNY's *chest he must have hooked his finger through its ring.*

HI

Reacting.

LENNY

Reacting to HI *reacting. He looks down.*

LENNY'S CHEST

On the bandoliers across his chest, silver pins glint in all the grenades—except one. Its squeeze-lever juts at a right angle from the grenade.

LENNY'S FACE

His jaw drops.

LENNY'S FEET

The lit cheroot hits the ground between his boots.

HI

Scrambling to his feet.

LENNY

Trying to drop the shotguns to free his hands. In his panic his fingers tangle in the trigger guards.

HI

Starting to run.

LENNY

Finally freeing his hands.

HI

Diving behind the parked car.

LENNY'S CHEST

His hands fly in to wrap around the grenade—too late— bright light:

LENNY

Blows sky-high. There is a roar as if the earth were cracking open and flame as if hell were slipping out.
   We pan the fire to the sky.
   Fade out.
   A white aluminum ladder rises up into the blackness, clanking softly. The top of the ladder arcs toward the camera.

JUMP BACK

To the interior of the Arizona second-story nursery as the ladder comes to rest against the window frame.
   It is late at night; the nursery is dark and empty.

THE HEADBOARD

*Of the unpainted crib with the burned-in names: Harry,
Barry, Larry, Garry, and Nathan Jr.*
   As we pull back from the headboard ED's *arms are gently
depositing the sleeping* NATHAN JR. *into the crib.* HI *puts the
singed copy of* Dr. Spock's Baby and Child Care *next to
the baby.*

REVERSE

HI *and* ED *looking sadly down at the baby.*
   *The silence is broken by the bleat of a squeeze-me toy as the
lights are snapped on.* HI *and* ED *turn, startled.*

NURSERY DOORWAY

NATHAN SR. *stands in his jammies, hair disheveled, holding a
gun and squinting against the light.*
   Keeping the gun trained on HI *and* ED, *he slowly raises a
pair of eyeglasses to his nose.*

NATHAN: The *hell* is goin' on?

*He advances cautiously into the nursery, gesturing with his
gun.*

   . . . Get away from there.

HI *and* ED *back away from the crib.*
   NATHAN *peers in and studies the baby for a moment.*
   *He lays the gun down, tenderly picks up the baby and
holds him to his chest. A tear forms at the corner of his eye.*
   HI *and* ED *are quietly moving back towards the ladder.*

NATHAN (*sharply*):   Waitaminute . . .

HI *and* ED *stop.*

. . . I ain't through with you. What're you doin' creepin' around here in the dark? You in with Smalls?

HI: . . . Scuse me?

As he bounces the baby, studying HI *and* ED:

NATHAN: Leonard Smalls, big fella rides a Harley, dresses like a rock star?

HI: No sir, that's who we saved him from. It's a long story.

NATHAN: Suppose you tell it.

HI: Well, sir, in a re-ward situation, they usually say no questions asked.

NATHAN: Do they.

HI shrugs.
  NATHAN turns to put the baby back in the crib.

. . . All right, boy, I guess you got a re-ward coming. Twenty thousand dollars . . .

He turns around with a thought:

NATHAN: . . . Or, if you need home furnishings, I can give you a line of credit at any of my stores. Fact, that's the way I'd rather handle it, for tax reasons . . .

HI: Well—

NATHAN throws his hands up in the air.

NATHAN: But it's up to you.

HI: Tell you the truth, I think we'd prefer the ca—

ED: We don't want no reward.

HI does a small take, surprised at this much integrity.

. . . We didn't bring him back for money.

NATHAN: Well, we could work it that way too.

ED: Could I just look at him a little bit more?

She stands looking into the crib. HI steps up next to her and puts an arm around her shoulder.

NATHAN: Be my guest, young lady . . . but would you mind tellin' me exactly how you—

ED starts crying softly as she gazes into the crib. HI murmurs something to comfort her.
NATHAN is studying the two of them.

. . . *You* took him, didn't you? Wasn't that biker a'tall.

HI turns to face him. He speaks in a rush.

HI: *I* took him, sir, my wife had nothin' to do with it. I crept in yon window and—

ED (*still crying*):   We both did it. We didn't wanna hurt him any; I just wanted to be a mama.

HI: It wasn't for money or nothin'. We just figured you had more'n you could handle, babywise. But I'm the one committed the actual crime sir, if you need to call the authorities—

NATHAN: Shutup boy, no one's callin' the authorities if there's no harm done.

HI: Thank you sir.

ED: Thank you sir.

NATHAN: Aw bullshit. Just tell me—just tell me why you did it.

ED: We can't have our own.

NATHAN looks at her. Finally he nods and sighs.

NATHAN: . . . Well lookit. If you can't have kids you gotta just keep tryin' and hope medical science catches up with you. Like Florence'n me—it caught up with a vengeance. And hell, even if it never does, you still got each other.

HI: Sir, those're kind words. But I think the wife and me are splittin' up . . .

He indicates ED with a nod of the head.

. . . Her point of view is we're both kinda selfish and unrealistic, so we ain't too good for each other.

NATHAN: Well ma'am, I don't know much but I do know human bein's. You brought back my boy so you must have your good points too. I'd sure hate to think of Florence leavin' me—I *do* love her so . . .

He clears his throat and turns to the door. His tone is harder again:

. . . You can go out the way you came in . . .

He snaps off the lights.

. . . And before you go off and do another foolish thing, like busting up, I suggest you sleep on it . . .

He has disappeared into the hall. We hear his voice receding:

. . . at least one night.

HIGH SHOT

Looking straight down at HI, *asleep in the trailer bedroom. We start to crane down.*

VO: That night I had a dream . . .

EXTREME WIDE SHOT

A beautiful dusk landscape. We are floating in over the field, abutting the prison, that GALE *and* EVELLE *popped out of.*
   In the middle background of the extreme long shot two men are walking across the field.

VO: . . . I dreamt I was as light as the ether, a floating spirit visiting things to come . . .

BACK TO HIGH SHOT   BEDROOM

Craning down toward HI.

VO: The shades and shadows of the people in my life wrastled their way into my slumber.

BACK TO FIELD

Still floating forward but now much closer to the two walking men. We see that they are GALE *and* EVELLE. *Both are still dyed blue.*
   They are approaching the hole in the ground.

VO: I dreamt that Gale and Evelle had decided to return to prison . . .

EVELLE is starting to climb into the hole.

. . . Probably that's just as well. I don't mean to sound superior, and they're a swell couple guys, but . . .

EVELLE has disappeared and GALE starts climbing in.

. . . maybe they weren't ready yet to come out into the world.

FLOATING UP THE WALK OF THE ARIZONA HOME

The front door has a holly wreath on it.

VO: And then I dreamed on, into the future, to a Christmas morn in the Arizona home . . .

DISSOLVE THROUGH TO:
ARIZONA LIVING ROOM

Five three-year-olds in their pyjamas are opening presents around a tree as NATHAN and FLORENCE look on.

VO: . . . where Nathan Jr. was opening a present from a kindly couple who preferred to remain unknown.

We have been isolating in on one of the children peeling the wrappings off a package marked TO NATHAN JR.
Inside is a shiny red plastic football.

FLOATING IN TOWARD A STATION WAGON

Pulled over on the state highway in the middle of the desert, a police motorcycle parked behind it. GLEN is leaning out the driver's window of the car talking to the state trooper who stands facing him.

vo: I saw Glen, a few years later, still havin' no luck gettin' the cops to listen to his wild tales about me'n Ed . . .

> GLEN *is grinning and talking with his hands cupped in front of him, as when he told* HI *about the Pollack who almost stepped in the pile of shit.*
> *The trooper, in crash helmet and dark sunglasses, is listening tight-lipped and stone-faced as* GLEN *finishes his story and slaps his knee.*

. . . Maybe he threw in one Pollack joke too many . . .

> *The trooper is clicking open his ballpoint pen and reaching his citation book from his breast pocket. The name tag on the pocket says "SGT. KOWALSKI."*

. . . I don't know.

FLOATING IN TOWARD A FOOTBALL

It sits on a tee in the middle of a football field.

vo: And still I dreamed on . . .

A cleated foot boots the football out of frame.

. . . further into the future than I'd ever dreamed before.

HIGH SCHOOL FOOTBALL PLAYER

Looking up, arms out at his sides, waiting to receive the kicked ball.

vo: . . . Watching Nathan Jr.'s progress from afar . . .

He catches the ball and starts running.

. . . Taking pride in his accomplishments as if he were our own . . .

He is skillfully eluding and stiff-arming tacklers.

. . . Wondering if he ever thought of us . . .

He reaches the end zone and triumphantly spikes the football.
  He whips off his helmet and we track in on the face of the rosy-cheeked high-school bruiser.

. . . and hoping that maybe we'd broadened his horizons a little, even if he couldn't remember just how they'd got broadened.

BACK TO BEDROOM

Still craning down, now very close to the sleeping HI.

VO: But still I hadn't dreamt nothin' about me'n Ed. Until the end . . .

DISSOLVE THROUGH TO:
A COUPLE

The man and woman are sitting on a sofa in the foreground with their backs to the camera. They are in the living room of HI *and* ED's *trailer, which is suffused with a warm golden light.*
  As they face the trailer's front door, all we see of the couple is the backs of their heads. They both have white hair, the woman's pulled into a bun. The old man wears a cardigan, the woman a shawl.

VO: . . . And this was cloudier 'cause it was years, years away.

The front door bursts open. Two young couples are entering as their kids—about a dozen of them—stream in around them.
  The old couple on the couch raise their arms to embrace their visitors. The children boil onto the couch.

. . . But I saw an old couple bein' visited by their children—and all their grandchildren too. And the old couple wasn't screwed up, and neither were their kids or their grandkids. And I don't know, you tell me. This whole dream, was it wishful thinking? Was I just fleein' reality, like I know I'm liable to do?

FLOATING IN TOWARD A LONG DINING TABLE

In the trailer. The table is all laid out with a Thanksgiving dinner, a huge turkey sitting at the far end.
  Cut-out letters at the other end of the room say: WELCOME HOME KIDS!
  The grandchildren are running into frame and taking their seats at the table, accompanied by their parents.

VO: . . . But me'n Ed, we can be good too . . .

The elderly couple enter from either side of the camera and stand in the foreground, backs to us, facing the table.

. . . And it *seemed* real. It *seemed* like us. And it seemed like . . . well . . . our home . . . If not Arizona, then a land, not *too* far away, where all parents are strong and wise and capable, and all children are happy and beloved. . . . I dunno, maybe it was Utah.

The elderly man drapes an arm around his wife's shoulder and draws her close.
  She rests her head against his shoulder, and we fade out.